W9-CKM-156

THE COMPLETE HISTORY OF

SHIPS AND BOATS

FROM SAILS AND OARS TO NUCLEAR-POWERED VESSELS

TRANSPORTATION AND SOCIETY

THE COMPLETE HISTORY OF

SHIPS AND BOATS

FROM SAILS AND OARS TO
NUCLEAR-POWERED VESSELS

EDITED BY ROBERT CURLEY , MANAGER, SCIENCE AND TECHNOLOGY

Britannica
Educational Publishing

IN ASSOCIATION WITH

ROSEN
EDUCATIONAL SERVICES

Published in 2012 by Britannica Educational Publishing
(a trademark of Encyclopædia Britannica, Inc.)
in association with Rosen Educational Services, LLC
29 East 21st Street, New York, NY 10010.

Distributed exclusively by Rosen Educational Services.
For a listing of additional Britannica Educational Publishing titles, call toll free (800) 237-9932.

First Edition

Britannica Educational Publishing
Michael I. Levy: Executive Editor
J.E. Luebering: Senior Manager
Marilyn L. Barton: Senior Coordinator, Production Control
Steven Bosco: Director, Editorial Technologies
Lisa S. Braucher: Senior Producer and Data Editor
Yvette Charboneau: Senior Copy Editor
Kathy Nakamura: Manager, Media Acquisition
Robert Curley: Manager, Science and Technology

Rosen Educational Services
Nicholas Croce: Rosen Editor
Nelson Sá: Art Director
Cindy Reiman: Photography Manager
Karen Huang: Photo Research
Brian Garvey: Designer
Matt Cauli: Cover Design
Introduction by Dan Faust

Library of Congress Cataloging-in-Publication Data

The complete history of ships and boats: from sails and oars to nuclear-powered vessels/ edited by Robert Curley.—1st ed.
    p. cm.—(Transportation and society)
"In association with Britannica Educational Publishing, Rosen Educational Services."
Includes bibliographical references and index.
ISBN 978-1-61530-670-1 (library binding)
1. Ships—History—Juvenile literature. 2. Shipbuilding—History—Juvenile literature. 3. Boats and boating—History—Juvenile literature I. Curley, Robert, 1955–
VM150.C625 2012
623.82009—dc23

                                                                    2011021362

Manufactured in the United States of America

On the cover: An Arleigh Burke-class guided-missile destroyer. *U.S.Navy photo by MC3c Crishanda K. McCall*

On pages x-xi: The hull of the amphibious assault ship USS *Bonhomme Richard*. *U.S. Navy photo by CMC Joe Kane*

Pages 1, 21, 40, 53, 75, 103, 118, 128, 150, 162, 165, 167 Shutterstock.com

CONTENTS

139

147

151

INTRODUCTION

I n today's world, if someone wanted to travel from New York City to San Francisco, all it would take would be a few hours on an airplane. Practically every corner of the planet is connected by the airline industry. However, it wasn't that long ago that governments rose and fell based solely upon the strength of their navy. Seventy-five percent of the Earth's surface is covered with water, so for thousands of years, ships and sailing were the key to a nation's wealth, expansion, and defense.

Archaeologists have shown us that the earliest civilizations grew up along the banks of rivers. These rivers provided a source of drinking water, irrigation for crops, and, in some cases, a source for wild game. In addition to these necessities, rivers could also provide a means of swift travel, especially in the centuries before well-established overland routes or well-maintained roads. Archaeological evidence in the form of clay tablets and containers reveals that boats have been in use since as early as 4000 BCE.

The earliest evidence of boats comes from Egypt. This should come as no surprise, considering the symbiotic relationship that the Egyptians had with the Nile. There are Egyptian hieroglyphs that depict massive barges being used to carry obelisks along the Nile. Some of these ships were as long as 100 metres (300 feet) and were larger than any warship built prior to the modern era. Egyptian boats used both oar and sail, and both needed to safely and effectively navigate the Nile.

Around 3000 BCE, the Egyptians ventured out to sea, voyaging across the Mediterranean Sea to Crete and Phoenicia. Both Crete and Phoenicia were civilizations built upon trade. As a result, Cretan and Phoenician ships were highly specialized and constructed to best facilitate maritime commerce.

When it comes to ship design, form follows function. In other words, a warship is designed differently from a cargo ship, which is designed differently from a passenger ship. This is true today and it was true three millennia ago. The earliest ships of the Mediterranean and Red Seas followed similar designs. Warships tended to be long and narrow, allowing for increased speed and maneuverability. Trading ships, however, needed to have as much space available for goods as possible, as well as needing higher sides to prevent flooding in the open seas. Of course, different geographic regions had notable differences in ship design. As the Roman Empire spread north, the Romans encountered ships that had different designs from what was common in the Mediterranean. The ships of northern Europe had an identical bow (front end) and stern (rear end), unlike their southern counterparts. More important, the ships that the Romans saw in the north relied almost entirely upon the use of sails. The sails of these northern ships made navigating the Atlantic Ocean possible, eventually leading to the Norse exploration of the New World several hundred years before the European Age of Exploration.

The switch from man-power to wind-power allowed for larger ships. Larger ships could travel farther and carry more goods, feeding the growth of overseas trade and, by extension, imperialism. Although the sail allowed for greater speed than rowing, the evolution of the sailing ship was an ongoing process. The earliest sailing ships utilized a single square sail that was often not highly maneuverable. As the centuries progressed, shipbuilders learned that a complex arrangement of sails of differing sizes and shapes that could be manipulated by the sailors to best catch the shifting winds would provide the best possible speed. Ships with more masts could carry more sails and, therefore, travel at greater speeds. For about 300 years, the standard sailing ships had two masts—one mast carried a large square sail, while the other carried a triangular one known as a lateen sail.

Changes to shipbuilding and sailing were slow during the Middle Ages. By this time, ships had evolved along two different paths: oar-driven galleys had become the dominant ship of war, while a sail-driven, two-masted vessel known as the buss became the main ship used for trade. The 13th and 14th centuries saw a number of changes to European shipbuilding and navigation due, in part, to cultural diffusion between East and West during the Crusades. For example, the steering oars common to European ships were soon replaced with a single rudder, which had been a common feature on Chinese junks for some time. Furthermore, advanced understanding of mathematics and astronomy allowed for better navigation. European sailors no longer needed to keep the coast in sight in order to accurately plot their course and location. This development opened up all of the world's oceans to European exploration and trade.

As the world got smaller, at least in the figurative sense, ships were getting larger. At the beginning of the 15th century, ships typically had three masts and carried five or six sails. During this time, trade between Europe and Asia was still carried out mostly through overland caravans. However, all that would change by the end of the century, after the famous voyages of Vasco Da Gama, Christopher Columbus, and John Cabot. As more nations started to compete in the new arena of global trade, ships had to get bigger. The increase in ship size was dictated by numerous factors. The most obvious reason for larger ships was the desire to hold more cargo, including supplies, which would reduce the number of times a ship would have to stop in port to restock provisions. Somewhat less obvious is the effect that size had on speed. The only way to increase the speed of a ship was for it to carry more sails, which required more masts. By the end of the 15th century, ships had more than doubled in size. Larger and faster ships became important as the nations of Western Europe—the Netherlands, England, France, Spain, and Portugal—began competing for economic superiority, both at home and in countries half-way around the world.

It should come as no surprise that commerce and imperialism are so closely linked. Overseas colonies provided two important components needed for a healthy economy back home: a source of raw materials and consumers clamouring for goods. Conflicts between nations became less about religion and politics and more about economics. The distinction that previously existed between ships used for trade and ships used for war disappeared. Merchant ships would often arm themselves in an attempt to fend off pirates, privateers, and business rivals. Over time, as the size and number of armament needed to defend a ship increased and the amount of cargo space decreased, merchant ships would forgo their own defence and travel in a convoy with armed naval vessels. The naval vessels of the 17th, 18th, and 19th centuries—known collectively as "ships of the line"— were very different from the small, oar-driven galleys once used as warships. Like their commercial counterparts, ships of the line were "full-rigged" ships—that is, they had three or more masts—that weighed several hundred tons. The similarities between merchant vessels and these new warships were not coincidental, since many of the larger naval vessels had started life as merchant ships. Fleets of these large, heavily-armed ships patrolled the trade routes, protecting both a nation's merchant fleets, and the wealth they produced, from its rivals. However, the supremacy of the sail-driven ship was about to come to an end.

By the middle of the 18th century, Britain was the undisputed ruler of the seas. British colonies in North

America, Africa, and Asia provided a steady stream of resources, goods, and gold. When the United States gained independence in 1783, it created an imbalance in the trade networks of the Northern Atlantic. The newly independent colonists no longer had access to British goods and Britain no longer had access to the timber and other resources of the former colonies. American merchants needed to find an alternate source of revenue, which led them to seek out markets in Asia and the Pacific. Britain suddenly found itself in direct economic competition with its own former subjects. America was a young nation and it needed an edge if it was going to compete against the greatest naval power in the world. American shipbuilders knew that the key was going to be speed—faster ships could deliver goods sooner and, in the case of perishable cargo, fresher. Although the Americans developed faster sailing ships—the clipper ships—the future of maritime travel would belong to the steamship.

The development of machine-powered ships is the final step between those simple Egyptian barges from 4000 BCE and the modern ships that can be seen in any port today. While the steam engine was first used to power small ships and ferries along the rivers and waterways of the eastern United States, the economic superiority of the railroad quickly removed steamboats from service. The next step was to perfect steam-powered navigation on the oceans. Once again the Americans and the British were in direct competition, with the North Atlantic as the field of battle. Although steam engines were faster than traditional sails, the ships themselves were still constructed from wood and, therefore, prone to damage caused by the powerful engines. Steamships would never be truly successful until the development of the iron hull.

With sail and timber replaced by steam and iron (and later steel), the 20th century saw the development of larger and faster ships than ever before: colossal container ships that can reach lengths of over 300 metres (1,000 feet), luxurious cruise ships, and massive aircraft carriers, often referred to as "floating military cities." It was the advances in shipbuilding, propulsion, and navigation that made these types of vessels possible. It should be noted that the "cruise" ship owes something of a debt to the rise of air travel. As airplanes grew in popularity and the transoceanic passenger trade dried up, many passenger liners were modified into the luxury liners of today. Steam engines gave way to increasingly more reliable diesel engines, gas turbines, electricity, and in, some cases, nuclear power. Further developments in automation also contributed to modern shipping procedures. Where it once took dozens of sailors and deckhands to tend to a ship's sails, masts, and riggings, a ship under mechanical propulsion only required a handful of crewmembers. The owners of merchant ships liked the idea of smaller crews, because it meant lower wages and fewer potential thieves.

Whether a ship is an ancient Egyptian barge, a Viking longship, or a modern container ship, they must all be built to follow the same basic scientific principles. An understanding of hydrostatics and hydrodynamics is key to shipbuilding. Put simply, hydrostatics comes down to the concept of buoyancy. For an object, in this case a ship, to remain afloat, its weight must be equal to the amount of water it displaces. The discovery of this principle is attributed to the Greek Archimedes (3rd century BCE); however, history shows us that ancient peoples understood the principle centuries before. Going hand-in-hand with hydrostatics is the principle of hydrodynamics, or the study of liquids in motion (and, by extension, the study of the motion of an object through a liquid). Effective sailing requires more than simply remaining afloat. Shipbuilders needed to understand the principles of hydrodynamics, even if they did not put a name to it, in order to craft hulls that would move swiftly and safely through the water. Although there are a number of different hull shapes that have been, and continue to be, used throughout the history of shipbuilding, the specific shape of a hull is dependent on a number of factors, including speed, stability, cargo requirements, and the types of waterways where the ship will be expected to operate.

While it may be tempting, from a 21st century point of view, to assume that ancient cultures lacked a modern scientific understanding of the world around them, an examination of the history of shipbuilding and sailing proves that is not the case. While they may not have written extensive and detailed theorems on the subjects, they were quite adept at observing the natural world and applying what they observed. Readers of this volume will not only discover the long history of sailing and ship design, but they will also discover just how advanced these ancient seafaring cultures truly were.

CHAPTER 1

THE AGE OF OAR AND SAIL

Surviving clay tablets and containers record the use of water-borne vessels as early as 4000 BCE, and the very fact that boats may be quite easily identified in 6,000-year-old illustrations shows how slow and continuous their evolution was until the mid-19th century, when steam propulsion became predominant. Indeed, some solutions to the problem of providing water transport were so successful and efficient several millennia ago that a number of boats are still in use whose origins are lost in prehistory.

EARLY ROWED VESSELS

The earliest historical evidence of boats is found in Egypt during the 4th millennium BCE. A culture nearly completely riparian, Egypt was narrowly aligned along the Nile, totally supported by it, and served by transport on its uninterruptedly navigable surface below the First Cataract (at modern-day Aswan). There are representations of Egyptian boats used to carry obelisks on the Nile from Upper Egypt that were as long as 100 metres (300 feet), longer than any warship constructed in the era of wooden ships.

The Egyptian boats commonly featured sails as well as oars. Because they were confined to the Nile and depended on winds in a narrow channel, recourse to rowing was essential. This became true of most navigation

An illustration of an early Nile boat featuring both sails and oars. 3LH-Fine Art/SuperStock/Getty Images

when the Egyptians began to venture out onto the shallow waters of the Mediterranean and Red seas. Most early Nile boats had a single square sail as well as one level, or row, of oarsmen. Quickly, several levels came into use, as it was difficult to maneuver very elongated boats in the open sea. The later Roman two-level bireme and three-level trireme were most common, but sometimes more than a dozen banks of oars were used to propel the largest boats.

Navigation on the sea began among Egyptians as early as the 3rd millennium BCE. Voyages to Crete were among the earliest, followed by voyages guided by landmark navigation to Phoenicia and, later, using the early canal that tied the Nile to the Red Sea, by trading journeys sailing down the eastern coast of Africa. According to the 5th-century-BCE Greek historian Herodotus, the king of Egypt about 600 BCE dispatched a fleet from a Red Sea port that returned to Egypt via the Mediterranean after a journey of more than two years. Cretan and Phoenician voyagers gave greater attention to the specialization of ships for trade.

The basic functions of the warship and cargo ship determined their design. Because fighting ships required speed, adequate space for substantial numbers of fighting men, and the ability to maneuver at any time in any direction, long, narrow rowed ships became the standard for naval warfare. In contrast, because trading ships sought to carry as much tonnage of goods as possible with as small a crew as practicable, the trading vessel became as round a ship as might navigate with facility. The trading vessel required increased freeboard (height between the water-line and upper deck level), as the swell in the larger seas could fairly easily swamp the low-sided galleys propelled by oarsmen. As rowed galleys became higher-sided and featured additional banks of oarsmen, it was discovered that the height of ships caused new problems. Long oars were awkward and quickly lost the force of their sweep. Thus, once kings and traders began to perceive the need for specialized ships, ship design became an important undertaking.

As was true of early wheeled vehicles, ship design also showed strong geographic orientation. Julius Caesar, for one, quickly perceived the distinctive, and in some ways superior, qualities of the ships of northern Europe. In the conquest of Britain and in their encounter with the Batavian area in Holland, Romans became aware of the northern European boat. It was generally of clinker construction (that is, with a hull built of overlapping timbers) and identical at either end. In the Mediterranean, ship design favoured carvel-built (that is, built of planks joined along their lengths to form a smooth surface) vessels that differed at the bow and stern (the forward and rear ends, respectively). In the early centuries, both Mediterranean and northern boats were commonly rowed, but the cyclonic storms found year-round in the Baltic and North Sea latitudes encouraged the use of sails. Because the sailing techniques of these early centuries depended heavily on sailing with a following wind (i.e., from behind), the frequent shifts in wind direction in the north permitted, after only relatively short waits, navigation in most compass directions. In the persistent summer high-pressure systems of the Mediterranean the long waits for a change of wind direction discouraged sailing. It was also more economical to carry goods by ship in the north. With a less absolute dependence on rowing, the double-ended clinker boat could be built with a greater freeboard than was possible in the rowed galleys of the Mediterranean. When European sailors began to look with increasing curiosity at the seemingly boundless Atlantic Ocean, greater freeboard made oceanic navigation more practicable.

THE FIRST SAILING SHIPS

The move to the pure sailing ship came with small but steadily increasing technical innovations that more often allowed ships to sail with the wind behind them. Sails changed from a large square canvas suspended from a single yard (top spar), to complex arrangements intended to pivot on the mast depending on the direction and force of the wind. Instead of being driven solely by the wind direction, ships could "sail into the wind" to the extent that the course taken by a ship became the product of a resolution of forces (the actual wind direction and the objective course of the particular ship). Sails were devised to handle gentle breezes and to gain some mileage from them as well as from strong winds and to maintain some choice as to course while under their influence.

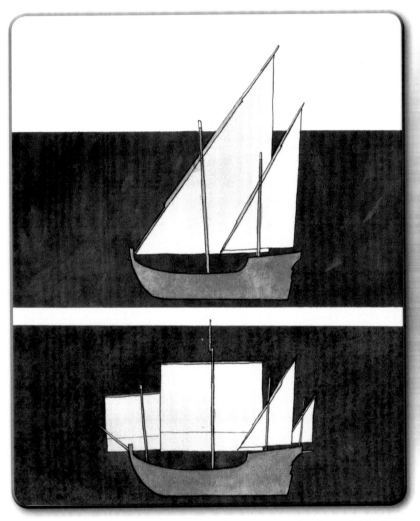

Lateen and square-rigged sails on a 15th-century ship. Richard Schlecht/ National Geographic Image Collection/Getty Images

TYPES OF SAILS

While the speed of a rowed ship was mainly determined by the number of oarsmen in the crew, in sailing ships the total spread of canvas in the sails was the main determinant of speed. Because winds are not fixed either as to direction or as to force, gaining the maximum effective propulsion from them requires complexly variable sails. There was one constant that characterized navigation by sail throughout its history—to gain speed it was necessary to increase the number of masts on the ship. Ships in both the Mediterranean and the north were single-masted until about 1400 CE and likely as well to be rigged for one basic type of sail. With experience square sails replaced the simple lateen sails that were the mainstay during the Middle Ages, particularly in the Mediterranean.

In the earlier centuries of sailing ships the dominant rig was the square sail, which features a canvas suspended on a boom, held aloft by the mast, and hung across the longitudinal axis of the ship. To utilize the shifting relationship between the desired course of the ship and the present wind direction, the square sail must be twisted on the mast to present an edge to the wind. Among other things this meant that most ships had to have clear decks amidships to permit the shifting of the sail and its boom; most of the deck space was thus monopolized by a single swinging sail. Large sails also required a sizable gang of men to raise and lower the sail (and, when reef ports were introduced, to reef the sail, that is, to reduce its area by gathering up the sail at the reef points).

By 1200 the standard sailing ship in the Mediterranean was two-masted, with the foremast larger and hung with a sail new to ordinary navigation at sea. This was the lateen sail, earlier known to the Egyptians and sailors of the eastern Mediterranean. The lateen sail is triangular in shape and is fixed to a long yard mounted at its middle to the top of the mast. The combination of sails tended to change over the years, though the second mast often carried a square sail.

One broad classification of sails, which included the lateen, was termed "fore-and-aft" sails—that is, those capable of taking the wind on either their front or back surfaces. Such sails are hung along the longitudinal axis of the ship. By tacking to starboard (the right side) the ship would use the wind from one quarter. Tacking to port (the left side) would use a wind coming from the opposite quarter to attain the same objective.

ASIAN SHIPS

During this same period China, with its vast land areas and poor road communications, was turning to water for transportation. Starting with a dugout canoe, the Chinese joined two canoes with planking, forming a square punt, or raft. Next, the side, the bow, and the stern were built up with planking to form a large, flat-bottomed wooden box. The bow was sharpened with a wedge-shaped addition below the waterline. At the stern, instead of merely hanging a steering oar over one side as did the Western ships, Chinese shipbuilders contrived a watertight box, extending through the deck and bottom, that allowed the steering oar or rudder to be placed on the centreline, thus giving better control. The stern was built to a high, small platform at the stern deck, later called a castle in the West, so that, in a following sea, the ship would remain dry. Thus, in spite of what to Western eyes seemed an ungainly figure, the Chinese junk was an excellent hull for seaworthiness as well as for beaching in shoal (shallow) water. The principal advantage, however, not apparent from an external view, was great structural rigidity. In order to support the side and the bow planking, the Chinese used solid planked walls (bulkheads), running both longitudinally and transversely and dividing the ship into 12 or more compartments, producing not only strength but also protection against damage.

In rigging the Chinese junk was far ahead of Western ships, with sails made of narrow panels, each tied to a sheet (line) at each end so that the force of the wind could be taken in many lines rather than on the mast alone; also, the sail could be hauled about to permit the ship to sail somewhat into the wind. By the 15th century junks had developed into the largest, strongest, and most seaworthy ships in the world. Not until about the 19th century did Western ships catch up in performance.

EARLY OCEANIC NAVIGATION

Richard I, Coeur de Lion (1157–1199), King of England, Duke of Normandy. Hulton Archive/Getty Images

The rise of oceanic navigation began when the basic Mediterranean trading vessel, the Venetian buss (a full-bodied, rounded two-masted ship), passed through the Strait of Gibraltar. At the time of Richard I of England (reigned 1189–99), whose familiarity with Mediterranean shipping stemmed from his participation in the Crusades, Mediterranean navigation had evolved in two directions: the galley had become a rowed fighting ship and the buss a sail-propelled trader's vessel. From Richard's crusading expeditions the value of the forecastle and aftercastle—giving enclosed deck houses and a bulging bow of great capacity—was learned, and this style became the basis of the English oceangoing trader. These crusading voyages also introduced the English to journeys longer than the coasting and North Sea navigation they had previously undertaken.

The story of European navigation and shipbuilding is in large part one of interaction between technical developments in the two narrow boundary seas. It is thought that sailors from Bayonne in southwestern France introduced the Mediterranean carrack (a large three-masted, carvel-build ship using both square and lateen sails) to northern Europe and in turn introduced the double-ended clinker ship of the north to the Mediterranean. This crossfertilization took place in the 14th century, a time of considerable change in navigation in the Atlantic-facing regions of France, Spain, and Portugal.

Changes in shipbuilding during the Middle Ages were gradual. Among northern ships the double-ended structure began to disappear when sailing gained dominance over rowing. To make best use of sails meant moving away from steering oars to a rudder, first attached to the side of the boat and then, after a straight stern post was adopted, firmly attached to that stern. By 1252 the Port Books of Damme in Flanders distinguished ships with rudders on the side from those with stern rudders.

The arts of navigation were improving at the same time. The compass was devised at the beginning of the 14th century, but it took time to understand how to use it effectively in a world with variable magnetic declinations. It was only about the year 1400 that the lodestone began to be used in navigation in any consistent manner.

The fleet of Christopher Columbus approaching the New World. Lambert/ Archive Photos/Getty Images

15TH-CENTURY SHIPS AND SHIPPING

The early 15th century saw the rise of the full-rigged ship, which had three masts and five or six sails. At the beginning of that century Europe and Asia were connected by caravan routes over land. The galleys or trade ships were long, low-sided, commonly rowed for much of their voyage, and guided by successive landfalls with little need for the compass and mathematical navigation. By the end of the century Da Gama, Columbus, and Cabot had made their revolutionary journeys, the Portuguese had organized the first school of oceanic navigation, and trade had begun to be global.

"Full-rigged" ships were introduced because trade was becoming larger in scale, more frequent in occurrence, and more distant in destination. There was no way to enlarge the propulsive force of ships save by increasing the area of sail. To pack more square yards of canvas on a hull required multiple masts and lofting more and larger sails on each mast. As multiple masts were added, the hull was elongated; keels were often two and a half times as long as the ship's beam (width). At the beginning of the 15th century large ships were of about 300 tons; by 1425 they were approximately 720 tons.

In the 16th century the full-rigged ship was initially a carrack, a Mediterranean three-master perhaps introduced from Genoa to England. The trade between the Mediterranean and England was carried on at Southampton largely by these carracks. As the years passed the galleon became the most distinctive vessel. This was most commonly a Spanish ship riding high out of the water. Although the name suggested a large galley, galleons probably never carried oars and were likely to be four-masted.

In earlier centuries ships were often merchantmen sufficiently armed to defend themselves against pirates, privateersmen, and the depredations of an active enemy. In peacetime a ship would go about its business as a nation's trader, but it was able to become a fighting vessel if necessary. When the size of guns and the numbers involved grew to create an offensive capability, there remained little space to carry the volume of goods required by a trader. What resulted was the convoy, under which merchantmen would be protected by specialized naval ships. The distinction between warship and trading ship might have remained quite abstract had not the theory and tactics of warfare changed. Most medieval wars were either dynastic or religious, and armies and navies were small by modern standards. But beginning with the warfare between the Dutch and the English in the 17th century, conflict was the result of competition in trade rather than in sovereignty and faith. Thus, the major trading nations came to dominate ship design and construction.

17TH-CENTURY DEVELOPMENTS

With the emergence of the eastern trade in about 1600 the merchant ship had grown impressively. The Venetian buss was rapidly supplanted by another Venetian ship, the cog. A buss of 240 tons with lateen sails was required by maritime statutes of Venice to be manned by a crew of 50 sailors. The crew of a square-sailed cog of the same size was only 20 sailors. Thus began an effort that has characterized merchant shipping for centuries—to reduce crews to the minimum. This was particularly true of oceanic navigation, because larger crews were expensive to pay and to provision—and the large amounts of provisions necessary were sometimes critical on long voyages.

In the north, vessels were commonly three-masted by the 16th century. These were the ships that Cabot used to reach Newfoundland and Drake, Frobisher, and Raleigh sailed over the world's oceans. Raleigh wrote that the Dutch ships of the period were so easy to sail that a crew one-third the size used in English craft could operate them. Efforts were made to accomplish technical improvements on English copies of Venetian and Genoese traders. These ultimately resulted in the East Indiaman of the 17th century. This large and costly ship was intended to be England's entry in a fierce competition with the Dutch for the trade of India and the Spice Islands.

When Europeans began to undertake trading voyages to the East, they encountered an ancient and economically well-developed world. In establishing a sea link with the East, European merchants could hope to get under way quickly using the producers already resident there and the goods in established production. What resulted were European "factories," settlements for trade established on coasts at places such as Bombay, Madras, and Calcutta. Some European merchants settled there, but there was no large-scale migration; production of the goods followed established procedures and remained in Asian hands. In contrast, in the New World of America and Australia there was so little existing production of trading goods that the establishment of ties required not only the pioneering of the trading route but also the founding of a colony to create new production. Shipping was critical in each of these relationships but became larger and more continuous in the case of the colonies.

Competition was fierce among the Europeans for the riches of the overseas trade. As the voyages were frequently undertaken by trading consortia from within the chartered company, a great deal is known about the profits of individual round-trips. Standard profits were 100 percent or more. In the accumulation of capital, by countries and by individuals, this mercantile activity was of the utmost importance. Holland's "Golden Century" was the 17th, and England's overtaking of France as Europe's seat of industry also occurred then. The English realized quickly that their merchant ships had to carry enough cannon and other firepower to defend their factories at Bombay and elsewhere and to ward off pirates and privateers on the long voyage to and from the East. In India the English contested trading concessions particularly with France and Portugal; in the East Indian archipelago the contest was with the Dutch and the Portuguese; and in China it was with virtually all maritime powers in northern and western Europe. The result was that the East

India merchantmen were very large ships, full-rigged and multimasted, and capable of sailing great distances without making a port.

To secure the strength and competence of these great merchant ships, advances in shipbuilding were necessary. The money was there: profits of 218 percent were recorded over five years, and even 50 percent profit could be earned in just 20 months. Among those undertaking more scientific construction was the British shipbuilder Phineas Pett (1570–1647). Much fine shipbuilding emerged, including ships of the English East India Company, but the company began to freeze its designs too early, and its operating practices were a combination of haughty arrogance and lordly corruption. Captains were appointed who then let out the functioning command to the highest bidder. Education was thin, treatment of sailors despicable, and reverence for established practice defeated the lessons of experience. The merchantmen had to carry large crews to have available the numbers to make them secure against attack. But lost in this effort for security was the operating efficiency that a sound mercantile marine should seek.

It was left more to other maritime markets to develop improvements in merchantmen after the early 17th century. The Dutch competitors of England were able to build and operate merchant ships more cheaply. In the 16th century the sailing ship in general service was the Dutch fluyt, which made Holland the great maritime power of the 17th century. A long, relatively narrow ship designed to carry as much cargo as possible, the fluyt featured three masts and a large hold beneath a single deck. The main and fore masts carried two or more square sails and the third mast a lateen sail. Only at the conclusion of the century, when the Dutch had been decisively defeated in the Anglo-Dutch trading wars, did England finally succeed to the role of leading merchant marine power in the world.

A John Marshall engraving of the Mayflower. © SuperStock

That role was gained in part because Oliver Cromwell restricted English trade to transport in English craft. In 1651 laws were initiated by Cromwell to deal with the low level of maritime development in England. The so-called Navigation Act sought to overcome conditions that had originated in the late Middle Ages when the Hanseatic League, dominating trade in the Baltic and northern Europe, carried most of Britain's foreign seaborne trade. When the Hansa declined in power in the 16th century the Dutch, just then beginning to gain independence from Spain politically and from Portugal in trade, gained a major part of the English carrying trade. The Navigation Act initiated a rapid change in that pattern. After the restoration of the Stuart monarchy, English shipping nearly doubled in tonnage between 1666 and 1688. By the beginning of the 18th century Britain had become the greatest maritime power and possessed the largest merchant marine until it lost that distinction to the Americans in the mid-19th century.

A further factor in the growth of national merchant marines was the increasing enforcement of the law of cabotage in the operations of the mercantile powers of northern and western Europe with respect to their rapidly expanding colonial empires. Cabotage was a legal principle first enunciated in the 16th century by the French. Navigation between ports on their coasts was restricted to French ships; this principle was later extended to apply to navigation between a metropolitan country and its overseas colonies. This constituted a restriction of many of the world's trade routes to a single colonial power. It became clear that a power seeking an advantage in shipping would be amenable to supporting the cost and fighting that gaining such colonies might require.

Geographic knowledge gained economic and political value in these conditions. It was in the 17th century that the Dutch, the French, and the English began trying to fill out the map of the known oceans. Islands and coastlines were added to sailing charts almost on an annual basis. By the mid-18th century all the world's shorelines not bound by sea ice, with fairly minor exceptions, were charted. Only Antarctica remained hidden until the mid-19th century.

SHIPPING IN THE 19TH CENTURY

Once the extent and nature of the world's oceans was established, the final stage of the era of sail had been reached. American independence played a major role in determining how the final stage developed.

To understand why this was so, it should be appreciated that Britain's North American colonies were vital to its merchant marine, for they formed a major part of its trading empire as customers for British goods. Under mercantilist economic doctrine, colonies were intended as a source of raw materials and as a market for manufactured goods produced in the metropolitan country. Maine, New Hampshire, Nova Scotia, and New Brunswick were rich in naval stores and timber for inexpensive hulls, masts, and spars. And the Navigation Act as amended also granted to the merchant fleets in British North America a monopoly on the transport of goods and passengers within the British Empire. When the United States became independent in 1783 the former colonies were rigidly denied access to the British metropolitan and colonial markets. The substantial trade that had tied Boston to Newfoundland and the British West Indies was severed, leaving the Americans to find an alternative trading system as quickly as possible. New England and the Middle Atlantic states, where there were significant fleets of sailing ships, turned to the Atlantic and Mediterranean islands as well as to

THE CUTTY SARK

The *Cutty Sark* was a three-masted British clipper ship, launched at Dumbarton, Scot., in 1869. It was 64.7 metres (212 feet 5 inches) long and 11 metres (36 feet) wide, and it had a net tonnage of 921. The name (meaning "short shirt") came from the garment worn by the witch Nannie in Robert Burns's poem *Tam o'Shanter*. On Feb. 16, 1870, the *Cutty Sark* left London on its maiden voyage, sailing to Shanghai by way of the Cape of Good Hope. The vessel served in the English-Chinese tea trade through the 1870s, later in the Australian wool trade, and finally as a training ship. In 1957, fully restored, the ship was installed in a concrete dry berth near the River Thames at Greenwich, London, and was opened to the public by Queen Elizabeth II as a maritime relic and sailing museum. In 2006 the *Cutty Sark* was closed for extensive renovations. The following year it was severely damaged by fire, but renovation work continued toward the goal of reopening the ship in time for the 2012 Summer Olympic Games in London.

Mauritius and to China. In this way, the merchants in the American ports created direct competition to the British East India Company. In doing so, they needed ships that could sail in the Far Eastern trade without the protection of the British navy and that could operate more efficiently and economically than those of the East India Company.

The British East Indiamen were extravagantly expensive to build. Contracts for their construction were awarded by custom and graft. Captains were appointed by patronage rather than education or professional qualifications. And the journeys to Canton, China, from England in East Indiamen were slow in a trade where fast passages were of value, for example, in guarding the quality of the tea being carried. American merchants were fully aware of these failings of the company and its ships. They set out to gain a foothold in the trade through innovations, particularly after the East India Company's monopoly in Britain's China trade was abolished in 1833.

British shipping remained rather stagnant after the development of the East Indiaman in the 17th century. The Dutch became the innovators in the second half of the 17th century and maintained that status until the outbreak of the Napoleonic Wars. The British East India Company was paying £40 a ton for ships whereas other owners paid only £25. In the 19th century American shipbuilders studied basic principles of sail propulsion and built excellent ships more cheaply. They also studied how to staff and operate them economically. The Americans began to see that even larger ships (that is, longer in relation to breadth) could carry more sail and thereby gain speed and the ability to sail well under more types of winds. For perishable cargoes speed meant that these fast ships reached British and European markets before those of their competitors and with a product in better condition.

In the 25 years after 1815 American ships changed in weight from 500 to 1,200 tons and in configuration from a hull with a length 4 times the beam to one with a ratio of 5 ½ to 1. The faster and thus shorter journeys meant that the shipowner could earn back his investment in two or three years. The *Mayflower* had taken 66 days to cross the Atlantic in 1620. The Black Ball Lines' nine-year average as of 1825 was 23 days from Liverpool to New York City. Twenty years later Atlantic ships had doubled in size and were not credited as a success unless they had made at least a single east-bound dash of 14 days or less.

The culmination of these American innovations was the creation of a hull intended primarily for speed, which came with the clipper ships. Clippers were long, graceful three-masted ships with projecting bows and exceptionally large spreads of sail. The first of these, the

Rainbow, was built in New York in 1845. It was followed by a number of ships built there and in East Boston particularly intended for the China-England tea trade, which was opened to all merchant marines by the late 1840s. Subsequently the *Witch of the Wave* (an American clipper) sailed from Canton to Deal in England in 1852 in just 90 days. Similar feats of sailing were accomplished in Atlantic crossings. In 1854 the *Lightning* sailed 701 km (436 miles) in a day, at an average speed of 18 ½ knots.

By 1840, however, it was clear that the last glorious days of the sailing ship were at hand. Pure sailing ships were in active use for another generation, while the earliest steamships were being launched. But by 1875 the pure sailer was disappearing, and by the turn of the 20th century the last masts on passenger ships had been removed.

CHAPTER 2

THE RISE OF MACHINE POWER

The key to machine-powered ships was the creation of a more efficient steam engine. Early engines were powered by steam at normal sea-level atmospheric pressure (approximately 101.35 kilopascals, or 14.7 pounds per square inch), which required very large cylinders. The massive engines were thus essentially stationary in placement. Any attempt to make the engine itself mobile faced this problem.

THE STEAMBOAT

This cumbersome quality of early 19th-century steam engines led to their being used first on ships. In the beginning the discordant relationship of machine weight to power production was a problem, but the ability to enlarge ships to a much greater size meant that the engines did not have to suffer severe diminution. A real constraint was the pattern of natural waterways; early steamboats for the most part depended on paddles to move the vessel, and it was found that those paddles tended to cause surface turbulence that eroded the banks of a narrow waterway, as most of the inland navigation canals were. Thus, the best locale for the operation of steamboats was found to be on fairly broad rivers free of excessively shallow stretches or rapids. A further consideration was speed. Most of the early experimental steamboats were very slow, commonly in the range of three or four miles per hour. At such speeds there was a considerable advantage redounding to coaches operating on well-constructed roads, which were quite common in France and regionally available in England.

The ideal venue for steamboats seemed to be the rivers of the eastern United States. Colonial transportation had mainly taken place by water, either on the surfaces of coastal bays and sounds or on fairly broad rivers as far upstream as the lowest falls or rapids. Up to the beginning of the 19th century a system of coastal and inland navigation could care for most of the United States' transportation needs. If a successful steamboat could be developed, the market for its use was to be found in the young, rapidly industrializing country.

EARLY EXAMPLES

The question of the invention of the steamboat raises fierce chauvinistic claims, particularly among the British, French, and Americans, but there seems to be broad agreement that the first serious effort was carried out by a French nobleman, Claude-François-Dorothée, Marquis de Jouffroy d'Abbans, on the Doubs River at Baum-des-Dames in the Franche-Comté in 1776. This trial was not a success, but in 1783 Jouffroy carried out a second trial with a much larger engine built three years earlier at Lyon. This larger boat, the *Pyroscaphe*, was propelled by two paddle wheels, substituted for the two "duck's feet" used in the previous trial. The trial took place on the gentle River Saône at Lyon, where the overburdened boat of 148,000 kg (327,000 pounds) moved against the current for some 15 minutes before it disintegrated from the pounding of the engines. This was unquestionably the first steam-powered boat to operate. There were subsequent French experiments, but further development of the steamboat was impeded by the French Revolution.

Illustration of an early version of John Fitch's steamboat. Library of Congress, Washington, D.C.

In the eastern United States James Rumsey, the operator of an inn at the Bath Springs spa in Virginia (later West Virginia), sought to interest George Washington in a model steamboat he had designed. On the basis of Washington's support, Virginia and Maryland awarded Rumsey a monopoly of steam navigation in their territories.

At the same time, another American, John Fitch, a former clockmaker from Connecticut, began experimenting with his vision of a steamboat. After much difficulty in securing financial backers and in finding a steam engine in America, Fitch built a boat that was given a successful trial in 1787. By the summer of 1788 Fitch and his partner, Henry Voight, had made repeated trips on the Delaware River as far as Burlington, 32 km (20 miles) above Philadelphia, the longest passage then accomplished by a steamboat.

British inventors were active in this same period. Both Rumsey and Fitch ultimately sought to advance their steamboats by going to England, and Robert Fulton spent

Clyde Canal in Falkirk, Scot. © www.istockphoto.com/David McCready

more than a decade in France and Britain promoting first his submarine and later his steamboat. In 1788 William Symington, son of a millwright in the north of England, began experimenting with a steamboat that was operated at five miles per hour, faster than any previous trials had accomplished. He later claimed speeds of roughly 10.5 and 11 km (6.5 and 7 miles) per hour, but his steam engine was thought too weak to serve, and for the time his efforts were not rewarded. In 1801 Symington was hired by Lord Dundas, a governor of the Forth and Clyde Canal, to build a steam tug; the *Charlotte Dundas* was tried out on that canal in 1802. It proved successful in pulling two 70-ton barges the 31 km (19.5 miles) to the head of the canal in six hours. The governors, however, fearing bank erosion, forbade its use on that route, and British experiments failed to lead further for some years.

FULTON'S STEAMBOAT

Instead, Robert Fulton, an American already well-known in Europe, began to gain headway in developing a steamboat. British historians have tended to deny his contributions and assign them to his supposed piracy of British inventions. It has been shown that he could not have pirated the plans of the *Charlotte Dundas*, but the record remains largely uncorrected. Fulton's "invention" of the steamboat depended fundamentally on his ability to make use of James Watt's patents for the steam engine, as Fitch could not. Having experimented on steamboats for many years, by the first decade of the 19th century Fulton had determined that paddle wheels were the most efficient means of propelling a boat, a decision appropriate to the broad estuarine rivers of the Middle Atlantic states. Fulton had built and tested on Aug. 9, 1803, a steamboat that ran four times to the Quai de Chaillot on the Seine River in Paris. As it operated at no more than 4.6 km (2.9 miles) per hour—slower than a brisk walk—he considered these results at best marginal.

Fulton returned to the United States in December 1806 to develop a successful steamboat with his partner Robert Livingston. A monopoly on steamboating in New York State had been previously granted to Livingston, a wealthy Hudson Valley landowner and American minister to France. On Aug. 17, 1807, what was then called simply the "North River Steamboat" steamed northward on the Hudson from the state prison. After spending the night at Livingston's estate of Clermont (whose name has ever since erroneously been applied to the boat itself) the "North River Steamboat" reached Albany eight hours later after a run at an average speed of 8 km (5 miles) per hour (against the flow of the Hudson River). This was a journey of such length and relative mechanical success that there can be no reasonable question it was the first unqualifiedly successful steamboat trial. Commercial service began immediately, and the boat made one and a half round-trips between New York City and Albany each week. Many improvements were required in order to establish scheduled service, but from the time of this trial forward Fulton and Livingston provided uninterrupted service, added steamboats, spread routes to other rivers and sounds, and finally, in 1811, attempted to establish steamboat service on the Mississippi River.

The trial on the Mississippi was far from a success but not because of the steamboat itself. Fulton, Livingston, and their associate Nicholas Roosevelt had a copy of their Hudson River boats built in Pittsburgh as the *New Orleans*. In September 1811 it set sail down the Ohio River, making an easy voyage as far as Louisville, but as a deep-draft estuarine boat it had to wait there for the flow of water to rise somewhat. Finally, drawing no more than 12.5 cm (5 inches) less than the depth of the channel, the New Orleans headed downriver. In an improbable coincidence, the steamboat came to rest in a pool below the Falls of the Ohio just before the first shock was felt of the New Madrid earthquake, the most severe temblor ever recorded in the United States. The earthquake threw water out of the Ohio and then the Mississippi, filling the floodplain of those rivers, changing their channels significantly, and choking those channels with uprooted trees and debris. When the *New Orleans* finally reached its destination it was not sent northward again on the service for which it had been built. Steamboats used on the deeper and wider sounds and estuaries of the northeastern United States were found to be unsuited to inland streams, however wide. Eventually boats drawing no more than 23–30 cm (9–12 inches) of water proved to be successful in navigating the Missouri River westward into Montana and the Red River into the South; this pattern of steamboating spread throughout much of interior America, as well as the interior of Australia, Africa, and Asia.

COMMERCIAL STEAM NAVIGATION

From the onset of successful inland steam navigation in 1807, progress was quite rapid. Fulton's steamboats firmly established Livingston's monopoly on the Hudson and adjacent rivers and sounds. Another experimenter, John Stevens, decided to move his steamboat *Phoenix* from the Hudson to the Delaware River. In June 1809, a 240-km (150-mile) run in the ocean between Perth Amboy, N.J., and Delaware Bay was the first ocean voyage carried out by a steamboat. Subsequently other coasting voyages were used to reach by sea the south Atlantic coast of the United States to Charleston, S.C., and Savannah, Ga. Slowly

and tentatively voyages along narrow seas were undertaken, and more countries became involved with steam
navigation.

The first commercial steam navigation outside the
United States began in 1812 when Henry Bell, the propri-
etor of the Helensburg Baths located on the Clyde below
Glasgow, added a steamboat, the *Comet*, to carry his customers from the city. It was followed soon after by others
steaming to the western Highlands and to other sea lochs.
One of these, the *Margery*, though built on the Clyde in
1814, was sent to operate on the Thames the next year;
but so much difficulty was encountered from established
watermen's rights on that stream that the boat was transferred in 1816 to French ownership and renamed the *Elise*.
It competed with Jouffroy's *Charles-Philippe* in service on
the Seine. Because of the generally more stormy nature of
Europe's narrow seas these steaming packets were generally small and cramped but capable of crossing waters
difficult for the American river steamboats to navigate.

The early 19th-century steamboat experiments were
aimed primarily at building and operating passenger ships.
Endowed with the Mississippi-Ohio-Missouri river system, the St. Lawrence–Great Lakes system, the Columbia
and its tributaries, and the Colorado system, North
America had virtually ideal conditions for the creation of
an extensive, integrated network of inland navigation by
shallow-draft steamboats. There was a strong geographic
expansion under way in Canada and the United States
that would be more quickly advanced by steamboats than
by land transportation. North American transportation
before the late 1850s was by river in most regions. This
was not a unique situation: most areas subject to 19th-cen-
tury colonization by Europeans—such as Siberia, South
America, Africa, India, and Australia—had a heavy dependence on river transport.

There were some mechanical improvements that encouraged this use of steamboats. Higher-pressure steam made craft more efficient, as did double- and triple-expansion engines. Improved hulls were designed. It was, however, the general level of settlement and economic productivity that tended to bring steamboat use to an end in inland transport. A demand for shipments of coal finally made the railroad the most economical form of transport and removed steamboats from many streams.

OCEANIC NAVIGATION

It was on the North Atlantic that most of the advances in steam shipping took place. Because river line and narrow-seas steaming was first to gain commercial importance, and shallow-water propulsion was easily accomplished with paddle wheels turning beside or behind the hull, that method of driving a ship was also the first to be used at sea.

THE FIRST ATLANTIC CROSSINGS

Oceanic steam navigation was initiated by an American coastal packet first intended entirely for sails but refitted during construction with an auxiliary engine. Built in the port of New York for the Savannah Steam Ship Company in 1818, the *Savannah* was 30 metres (98.5 feet) long with a 7.9-metre (25.8-foot) beam, a depth of 4.3 metres (14.2 feet), and a displacement of 320 tons. Owing to a depression in trade, the owners sold the boat in Europe where economically constructed American ships were the least expensive on the market and were widely seen as the most advanced in design. Unable to secure either passengers or cargo, the *Savannah* became the first ship to employ steam in crossing an ocean. At 5:00 in the morning on May 24, 1819, it set sail from Savannah. After taking on coal at

Kinsale in Ireland, it reached Liverpool on July 20, after 27 days and 11 hours; the engine was used to power the paddle wheels for 85 hours. Subsequently the voyage continued to Stockholm and St. Petersburg, but at neither place was a buyer found; it thus returned to Savannah, under sail because coal was so costly, using steam only to navigate the lower river to reach the dock at Savannah itself.

The next voyage across the Atlantic under steam power was made by a Canadian ship, the *Royal William*, which was built as a steamer with only minor auxiliary sails, to be used in the navigation of the Gulf of St. Lawrence. The owners, among them the Quaker merchant Samuel Cunard, of Halifax, N.S., decided to sell the ship in England. The voyage from Quebec to the Isle of Wight took 17 days. Soon thereafter, the *Royal William* was sold to the Spanish government. The ability to navigate the North Atlantic was demonstrated by this voyage, but the inability to carry any load beyond fuel still left the Atlantic challenge unmet.

THE "ATLANTIC FERRY"

At this point the contributions of Isambard Kingdom Brunel to sea transportation began. Brunel was the chief engineer of the Great Western Railway between Bristol and London, which was nearing completion in the late 1830s. A man who thrived on challenges, Brunel could see no reason his company should stop in Bristol just because the land gave out there. The Great Western Railway Company set up a Great Western Steamship Company in 1836, and the ship designed by Brunel, the *Great Western*, set sail for New York City on April 8, 1838. Thus began a flow of shipping that earned in the second half of the 19th century the sobriquet "the Atlantic Ferry" because of its scale and great continuity.

Illustration of the launch of the steamship Great Britain. Hulton Archive/ Getty Images

The Great Western Steamship Company, though the first major company organized, did not earn the pride of place one might have expected. Its next ship, the *Great Britain* of 1843, was the first with an all-iron hull; it has survived, now in the dry dock in which it was constructed in Bristol's Floating Dock, to this day. It was Cunard's steamboat company, however, that won the British government contract to establish a mail line across the North Atlantic. In 1840 the Cunard Line launched four paddle steamers with auxiliary sails—the *Britannia*, *Acadia*, *Columbia*, and *Caledonia*—which with their long line of successors became the leaders in a drive for speed and safety on the North Atlantic. From 1840 until the outbreak of the American Civil War the competition lay largely between the British lines and the American lines. During the war American shipping was greatly reduced as Confederate raiders, mostly constructed in Britain, either sank Union ships or drove them to operate under other registries. For a short period in the 1860s the United States went from being the world's largest merchant marine power to merely an importing shipping nation.

By the mid-1860s Britain had abandoned the paddle steamer for the Atlantic run, but the recently organized Compagnie Générale Transatlantique (known as the French Line in the United States) in 1865 launched the *Napoléon III*, which was the last paddle steamer built for the Atlantic Ferry. Early in the history of steam navigation the Swedish engineer John Ericsson had attempted unsuccessfully to interest the British Admiralty in the screw propeller he had invented. The U.S. Navy did adopt the propeller, however, and Ericsson moved to the United States. While there he also did pioneering work on the ironclad warship, which was introduced by the Union navy during the Civil War.

During the last third of the 19th century, competition was fierce on the North Atlantic passenger run. Steamship companies built longer ships carrying more powerful engines. Given the relatively large space available on a ship, the steam could be pressed to do more work through the use of double- and triple-expansion engines. That speed appealed greatly to the first-class passengers, who were willing to pay premium fares for a fast voyage. At the same time, the enlarged ships had increased space in the steerage, which the German lines in particular saw as a saleable item. Central Europeans were anxious to emigrate to avoid the repression that took place after the collapse of the liberal revolutions of 1848, the establishment of the Russian pogroms, and conscription in militarized Germany, Austria, and Russia. Because steamships were becoming increasingly fast, it was possible to sell little more than bed space in the steerage, leaving emigrants to carry their own food, bedding, and other necessities. Without appreciating this fact, it is hard to explain why a speed race led as well to a great rise in the capacity for immigration to the United States and Canada.

Steamship transportation was dominated by Britain in the latter half of the 19th century. The early efforts there had been subsidized by mail contracts such as that given to Cunard in 1840. Efforts by Americans to start a steamship line across the Atlantic were not notably successful. One exception was the Collins Line, which in 1847 owned the four finest ships then afloat—the *Arctic*, *Atlantic*, *Baltic*, and *Pacific*—and in 1851 the Blue Riband (always a metaphorical rank rather than an actual trophy) given for the speediest crossing of the New York–Liverpool route passed from Cunard's *Acadia* to the Collins *Pacific*, with the winning speed averaging 13 knots. The Collins Line, however, did not survive for long. Collision removed the *Arctic* from the line in 1854, and other losses followed. The contest was then mostly among British companies.

Most ships on the Atlantic were still wooden-hulled, so that the newer side-lever steam engines were too powerful for the bottoms in which they were installed, making maintenance a constant problem. Eventually the solution was found in iron-hulled ships. The size of ships was rapidly increased, especially those of Brunel. Under his aegis in 1858 a gigantic increase was made with the launching of the *Great Eastern*, with an overall length of 211 metres (692 feet), displacing 32,160 tons, and driven by a propeller and two paddle wheels, as well as auxiliary sails. Its iron hull set a standard for most subsequent liners, but its size was too great to be successful in the shipping market of the 1860s.

German ships of this period tended to be moderately slow and mostly carried both passengers and freight. In the late 1890s the directors of the North German Lloyd

Steamship Company entered the high-class passenger trade by construction of a Blue Riband-class liner. Two ships were ordered—the 1,749-passenger *Kaiser Wilhelm der Grosse* (199 metres, or 655 feet, long overall; displacement 23,760 tons), with twin screws, and the *Kaiser Friedrich*, which was returned to the builders having failed to meet speed requirements. When the *Kaiser Wilhelm der Grosse* won the Blue Riband on the eastbound leg of its third voyage in the fall of 1897, a real race broke out. North German Lloyd handled 28 percent of the passengers landed in New York City in 1898, so Cunard ordered two superliners, which represented the first steamers to be longer than the Great Eastern.

PASSENGER LINERS IN THE 20TH CENTURY

The upper limits of speed possible with piston-engined ships had been reached, and failure in the machinery was likely to cause severe damage to the engine. In 1894 Charles A. Parsons designed the yacht *Turbinia*, using a steam turbine engine with only rotating parts in place of reciprocating engines. It proved a success, and in the late 1890s, when competition intensified in the Atlantic Ferry, the question arose as to whether reciprocating or turbine engines were the best for speedy operation. Before Cunard's giant ships were built, two others—*Caronia* and *Carmania*—of identical size at 198 metres (650 feet) were fitted, respectively, with quadruple-expansion piston engines and a steam-turbine engine so that a test comparison could be made; the turbine-powered *Carmania* was nearly a knot faster. Cunard's giant ships, the *Lusitania* and the *Mauretania*, were launched in 1906. The *Lusitania* was sunk by a German submarine in 1915 with a great loss of life. The *Mauretania* won the Blue Riband in 1907 and held

The Titanic. The Bettmann Archive

it until 1929. It was perhaps the most popular ship ever launched until it was finally withdrawn in 1934.

The British White Star Line, which competed directly with Cunard, also had commissioned two giant liners. The *Olympic* of 1911, displacing 45,324 tons, was then the largest ship ever built. The *Titanic* of 1912 displaced 46,329 tons, so vast as to seem unsinkable. The *Titanic* operated at only 21 knots, compared with the *Mauretania*'s 27 knots, but its maiden voyage in 1912 was much anticipated. The ship collided with an iceberg off the Newfoundland coast and sank within hours, with a loss of about 1,500 lives.

World War I completely disorganized the Atlantic Ferry and in 1918 removed German competition. At that time Germany had three superliners, but all were taken as war reparations. The *Vaterland* became the U.S. Lines' *Leviathan*; the *Imperator* became the Cunard Line's *Barengaria*; and the *Bismarck* became the White Star Line's *Majestic*. That war severely cut traffic, although ships were used for troop transport. By eliminating German competition and seizing their great ships, the Western Allies returned to competing among themselves.

During the prosperous years of the 1920s, tourist travel grew rapidly, calling forth a new wave of construction, beginning with the French Line's *Île de France* in 1927 and gaining fiercer competition when the Germans returned to the race with the launching on successive days in 1928 of the *Europa* and the *Bremen*. But by the end of 1929 the Great Depression had begun; it made transatlantic passage a luxury that fewer and fewer could afford and rendered immigration to the United States impractical.

Because the international competition in transatlantic shipping reached full stride only with the return of German ships in 1928, major decisions as to construction were made just as the Great Depression was beginning. Since the beginning of the century the "1,000-foot" ship had been discussed among shipowners and builders. A new *Oceanic* was planned in the late 1920s but abandoned in 1929 because its engines seemed impractical. In 1930 the French Line planned a quadruple-screw liner of 299 metres (981.5 feet), which would represent another—and, as it turned out, the final—ratchet in the expansion of the passenger liner. What came of that undertaking was the most interesting, and by wide agreement the most beautiful, large ship ever built. The *Normandie* was the first large ship to be built according to the 1929 Convention for Safety of Life at Sea and was designed so the forward end of the promenade deck served as a breakwater, permitting it to maintain a high speed even in rough weather. The French Line had established a policy with the *Île de France* of encouraging tourist travel through luxurious accommodations (changing from third class, which was little more than steerage with private cabins, to tourist class, which was simple but comfortable). The *Normandie* offered seven accommodation classes in a total of 1,975

THE LUSITANIA

On May 7, 1915, the 32,000-ton British ocean liner *Lusitania* was returning from New York to Liverpool, with 1,959 passengers and crew onboard. The sinkings of merchant ships off the south coast of Ireland and reports of German submarine activity there had prompted the British Admiralty to warn the *Lusitania* to avoid the area and to recommend adopting the evasive tactic of zigzagging, changing course every few minutes at irregular intervals to confuse any attempt by U-boats to plot her course for torpedoing. The ship's crew chose to ignore these recommendations, and on the afternoon of May 7 the vessel was attacked. A torpedo struck and exploded amidships on the starboard side, followed by a heavier explosion, probably of the ship's boilers. Within 20 minutes the vessel had sunk, and 1,198 people were drowned. The loss of the liner and so many of its passengers, including 128 U.S. citizens, aroused a wave of indignation in the United States, and it was fully expected that a declaration of war would follow, but the U.S. government clung to its policy of neutrality.

The *Lusitania* was also carrying a cargo of rifle ammunition and shells (together about 173 tons), and the Germans, who had circulated warnings that the ship would be sunk, felt themselves fully justified in attacking a vessel that was furthering the war aims of their enemy. The German government also felt that, in view of the vulnerability of U-boats while on the surface and the British announcement of intentions to arm merchant ships, prior warning of potential targets was impractical. On May 13, 1915, the U.S. government sent a note to Berlin expressing an indictment of the principles on which the submarine war was being fought, but this note and two following ones constituted the immediate limit of U.S. reaction to the *Lusitania* incident. Later, in 1917, however, the United States did cite German submarine warfare as a justification for American entry into the war.

berths; the crew numbered 1,345. The ship popularized a design style, Moderne, that emulated the new, nonhistorical art and architecture. The bow was designed with the U-shape favoured by the designer Vladimir Yourkevitch. Turboelectric propelling machines of 160,000 shaft horsepower allowed a speed of 32.1 knots in trials in 1935. In 1937 it was fitted with four-bladed propellers, permitting a 3-day, 22-hour and 7-minute crossing, which won the Blue Riband from the *Europa*.

To compete with the *Normandie*, in 1930 Cunard built the *Queen Mary*, which was launched in 1934. At 297 metres (975 feet), it was Britain's first entry in the 1,000-foot category. The ship was never so elegant as its French rival and was a bit slower, but its luck was much better. The *Normandie* burned at the dock in New York in February 1942 while being refitted as a troopship. The *Queen Mary* was the epitome of the Atlantic liner before being retired to Long Beach, Calif., to serve as a hotel.

During World War II civilian transportation by sea was largely suspended, whereas military transport was vastly expanded. Great numbers of "Liberty" and "Victory" ships were constructed, and at the close of the war surplus ships were returned to peacetime purposes. A sister ship of the *Queen Mary*, the *Queen Elizabeth* (at 83,673 tons the largest passenger ship ever built), was launched in 1938, but the interior had not been fitted out before the war came in 1939. First used as a troopship during the war, it was completed as a luxury liner after 1945 and operated with the *Queen Mary* until the 1960s, when the jet airplane stole most of the trade from the Atlantic Ferry.

Experience with the two Cunard liners in the years immediately after 1945 suggested the value in having two giant ships, of approximately the same size and with a speed that allowed a transatlantic run of four days or less, so that one ship might sail from New York and another from Europe weekly. This competition began when U.S. Lines launched the 53,329-ton *United States*. Though lighter than the *Queen Elizabeth*, greater use of aluminum in the superstructure and more efficient steam turbine engines allowed it to carry essentially the same number of passengers. The great advantage lay in its speed of 35.59 knots, which captured the Blue Riband from the *Queen Mary* in 1952, an honour the latter had held for 14 years.

CARGO SHIPS

The history of other merchant marine activities parallels that of the great passenger liners. Freighter navigation, tanker navigation, naval ships, and, from the mid-20th century, the near replacement of bulk cargo by container transport must be understood as a similar ever-improving technology. Iron followed wood as a construction material and was followed in turn by steel. Until very recently steam was a source of power, though the diesel engine was used for some ships as early as the *Vandal* of 1903. After 1900 there was a general division between the use of steam turbines in passenger liners and diesel engines in freighters. Europeans, particularly the Scandinavians, favoured the diesel internal-combustion engine, with its more economical fuel consumption, whereas American shipping companies tended to favour steam turbines because their labour costs were usually lower. The rapid rise in the cost of petroleum fuel after 1973 led to increased diesel-engine construction, a trend that continued through subsequent decades.

CHAPTER 3

MODERN SHIP TYPES

The great majority of ships that are neither military vessels nor yachts can be divided into several broad categories: cargo carriers, passenger carriers, industrial ships, service vessels, and noncommercial miscellaneous. Each category can be subdivided, with the first category containing by far the greatest number of subdivisions.

SERVICE VESSELS

The service ships are mostly tugs or towing vessels whose principal function is to provide propulsive power to other vessels. Most of them serve in harbours and inland waters, and, because the only significant weight they need carry is a propulsion plant and a limited amount of fuel, they are small in size. The towing of massive drilling rigs for the petroleum industry and an occasional ocean salvage operation (e.g., towing a disabled ship) demand craft larger and more seaworthy than the more common inshore service vessels, but oceangoing tugs and towboats are small in number and in size compared to the overwhelmingly more numerous cargo ships.

MISCELLANEOUS

The word *miscellaneous* has only small scope here. It is intended to encompass classifications such as icebreakers and research vessels, many of which are owned by government. Neither type need be of large size, since no cargo is to be carried. However, icebreakers are usually wide in order to make a wide swath through ice, and they have high propulsive power in order to overcome the resistance of the ice layer. Icebreakers also are characterized by strongly sloping bow profiles, especially near the waterline, so that they can wedge their way up onto thick ice and crack it from the static weight placed upon it. To protect the hull against damage, the waterline of the ship must be reinforced by layers of plating and supported by heavy stiffeners.

Damage to propellers is also an icebreaking hazard. Propellers are usually given protection by a hull geometry that tends to divert ice from them, and they are often built with individually replaceable blades to minimize the cost of repairing damage. Electric transmission of power between engines and propellers is also common practice, since it allows precise control and an easy diversion of power to another propeller from one that may be jammed by chunks of broken ice.

Research vessels are often distinguished externally by cranes and winches for handling nets and small underwater vehicles. Often they are fitted with bow and stern side thrusters in order to enable them to remain in a fixed position relative to the Earth in spite of unfavourable winds and currents. Internally, research vessels are usually characterized by laboratory and living spaces for the research personnel.

INDUSTRIAL SHIPS

Industrial ships are those whose function is to carry out an industrial process at sea. A fishing-fleet mother ship that processes fish into fillets, canned fish, or fish meal is an example. Some floating oil drilling or production rigs are built in ship form. In addition, some hazardous industrial wastes are incinerated far at sea on ships fitted with the necessary incinerators and supporting equipment. In many cases, industrial ships can be recognized by the structures necessary for their function. For example, incinerator ships are readily identified by their incinerators and discharge stacks.

PASSENGER CARRIERS

Most passenger ships fall into two subclasses, cruise ships and ferries.

CRUISE SHIPS

Passenger cruise ship in the Panama Canal.
Joe Viesti/Viesti Associates, Inc.

Cruise ships are descended from the transatlantic ocean liners, which, since the mid-20th century, have found their services preempted by jet aircraft. Indeed, even into the 1990s some cruise ships were liners built in the 1950s and '60s that had been adapted to tropical cruising through largely superficial alterations—e.g., the addition of swimming pools and other amenities to suit warm-latitude cruising areas. However, most cruise ships now in service were built specifically for the cruise trade. Since most of them are designed for large numbers of passengers (perhaps several thousand), they are characterized by high superstructures of many decks, and, since their principal routes lie in warm seas, they are typically painted white all over. These two characteristics give them a "wedding cake" appearance that is easily recognizable from great distances. Closer examination usually reveals a large number of motor launches carried aboard for the ferrying ashore of passengers. Many cruise ships have stern ramps, much like those found on cargo-carrying roll-on/roll-off ships, in order to facilitate the transfer of passengers to the launches and to serve as docking facilities for small sporting boats.

The above features present the principal challenge to the cruise-ship designer: providing the maximum in safety, comfort, and entertainment for the passengers. Thus, isolation of machinery noise and vibration is of high importance. Minimizing the rolling and pitching motions of the hull is even more important—no extreme of luxury can offset a simple case of seasickness. Since cruising is a low-speed activity, propulsive power is usually much lower than that found in the old ocean liners. On the other hand, electrical power is usually of much greater magnitude, mainly because of demands by air-conditioning plants in tropical waters. The typical large cruise ship built since 1990 is powered by a "central station" electric plant—i.e., an array of four or more identical medium-speed diesel engines driving 60-hertz alternating-current electrical generators. This electrical plant supplies all shipboard power needs, including propulsion. Since all power flows from a single source, propulsion power can be readily diverted to meet increased air-conditioning loads while the ship is in port.

THE QUEEN ELIZABETH

Queen Elizabeth is the name given to three ships belonging to the British Cunard Line that successfully crossed over from the age of the transatlantic ocean liner to the age of the global cruise ship.

The first *Queen Elizabeth* was one of the largest passenger liners ever built. Launched in 1938 and used as a troopship during World War II, it entered the regular transatlantic service of the Cunard Line in 1946. The ship was 314 metres (1,031 feet) long and 36 metres (118.5 feet) wide and had a draft of 11.6 metres (38 feet) and an original gross tonnage of 83,673. The *Queen Elizabeth* was retired in 1968 and sold for conversion to a seagoing university, but it burned and sank in January 1972 during refitting at Hong Kong.

The Queen Elizabeth *entering New York City's harbour, c. 1945–47.*
Encyclopædia Britannica, Inc.

Its successor, the *Queen Elizabeth 2* (*QE2*), was launched in 1967 and made its maiden voyage between England and New York in 1969. The ship, 294 metres (963 feet) long and displacing 70,327 tons, was slightly smaller than its predecessor so that it could pass through the Panama Canal and operate as a cruise ship in addition to being a transatlantic liner. Its steam turbine engines gave it a top speed of 32.5 knots (though its service speed was 28.5 knots). In 1982 the *QE2* was requisitioned as a troop carrier in the Falkland Islands War. In 1986–87 the turbines were replaced with diesel engines. The *QE2* made its final voyage between New York and England in 2008 after having become the longest-serving ship in Cunard's history. Later that year the ship sailed to Dubai, where it was handed over to new owners for refitting as a floating hotel.

Cunard took delivery of a new *Queen Elizabeth* in 2010. Known variously as the *QE* and the *QE3*, the cruise ship was approximately the same length as the *QE2* but with a slightly greater displacement of more than 90,000 tons. Designed in an Art-Deco style to evoke memories of its predecessors and the great passenger liners of the pre-World War II era, the luxury ship could accommodate 2,000 passengers and 1,000 crewmembers on cruises to the Mediterranean, Caribbean, and other destinations around the world.

FERRIES

Ferries are vessels of any size that carry passengers and (in many cases) their vehicles on fixed routes over short cross-water passages. The building of massive bridges and tunnels has eliminated many ferry services, but they are still justified where waters are too formidable for fixed crossings. Vessels vary greatly in size and in quality of accommodations. Some on longer runs offer overnight cabins and even come close to equaling the accommodation standards of cruise ships. All vessels typically load vehicles aboard one or more decks via low-level side doors or by stern or bow ramps much like those found on roll-on/roll-off cargo ships.

A special type of ferry is the "double-ender," built for shuttling across harbour waters. The typical vessel has propellers, rudders, control stations, and loading ramps at both ends. It is usually wide enough to handle four vehicle lanes abreast and may accommodate up to 100 four-wheeled vehicles. Special docks, fitted with adjustable ramps to cope with changes in water levels and shaped to fit the ends of the ferry, are always part of a ferry system of this type.

Another special type of ferry is a high-speed vessel that in many cases is of catamaran (twin-hulled) design. This type is typically found on short runs in protected waters where the carriage of vehicles is not required. Catamaran hulls can be narrow and knifelike in shape, allowing them to operate at high speed-to-length ratios without excessive propulsive power. The engines are usually high-speed diesels, although turbine engines have been fitted in a few instances.

CARGO CARRIERS

Cargo ships can be distinguished by the type of cargo they carry, especially since the means of handling the cargo is often highly visible. The trend is toward specialization in this regard. One consequence is a proliferation in types of cargo vessels. The discussion below is limited to a few types that are represented by large numbers of ships and are distinctive in appearance.

TANKERS

Ships that carry liquid cargo (most often petroleum and its products) in bulk are made distinctive by the absence of cargo hatches and external handling gear. When fully loaded they are also readily distinguishable by scant freeboard—a condition that is permissible because the upper deck is not weakened by hatches. In essence, the tanker is a floating group of tanks contained in a ship-shaped hull, propelled by an isolated machinery plant at the stern. Each tank is substantially identical to the next throughout the length of the ship. The tanks are fitted with heating coils to facilitate pumping in cold weather. Within the tanks are the main, or high-suction, pipes, running several feet from the bottom to avoid sludge. Below them, low-suction piping, or stripping lines, removes the lowest level of liquid in the tank. Tanks are filled either through open trunks leading from the weather deck or from the suction lines with the pumps reversed. Because tankers, except for military-supply types, usually move a cargo from the source to a refinery or other terminal with few maneuvers en route, the machinery plant is called on only to produce at a steady rate the cruise power for the ship; consequently, considerable use of automatic controls is possible, thus reducing the size of the crew to a minimum. In view of the simplicity of inner arrangement, the tanker lends itself to mass production perhaps more than any other ship type. Because of the limited crew requirements and the low cost per ton for initial building and outfitting, the tanker has led the way in the rapid expansion in the size of ships. Rising crude oil prices in the late 20th century reinforced a trend toward greater tanker size, leading to the appearance of "supertankers," ships that reach 400 metres (1,300 feet) in length and a deadweight of 500,000 tons. Experience with supertankers has shown that the direct cost of transporting oil goes down as the size of the tanker increases, apparently without limit; an obstacle to building larger tankers is the lack of suitable shore facilities for them. Objection to these huge vessels has been raised by conservationists; when tankers suffer damage at sea, large oil spillages may result that can cause great damage to fish and other wildlife and to nearby coasts.

Along with the great increase in numbers and size of tankers have come specialized uses of tankers for products other than oil. A major user is the natural gas industry. For shipment, gas is cooled and converted to liquid at -162 °C (-260 °F) and is then pumped aboard a tanker for transit in aluminum tanks that are surrounded by heavy insulation to prevent absorption of heat and to keep the liquid from evaporating during the voyage. The cost of these ships is rather high, because steel cannot be used for the containers. The cold liquid, in contact with steel, would make that material as brittle as glass. Aluminum is therefore used, sometimes backed by balsa wood, backed in turn by steel. A special nickel-steel alloy known as Invar also has been used in this application.

CONTAINER SHIPS

Like tankers, container ships are characterized by the absence of cargo handling gear, in their case reflecting the

Front view of a container ship stacked high with containers above decks.
Shutterstock.com

usual practice of locating the container-handling cranes at shore terminals rather than aboard ship. Unlike the tanker, container ships require large hatches in the deck for stowing the cargo, which consists of standardized containers usually either 6 or 12 metres (20 or 40 feet) in length. Belowdecks, the ship is equipped with a cellular grid of compartments opening to the weather deck; these are designed to receive the containers and hold them in place until unloading is achieved at the port of destination. The ship is filled to the deck level with containers, the hatches are closed, and one or two layers of containers, depending upon the size and stability of the ship, are loaded on the hatch covers on deck.

In a few hours the ship can be filled with containers destined for another port and can be under way. An additional economy is the low cost of the crew of the ship while it is in port awaiting loading or unloading. Further, because each ship can make more trips than before, container fleets require fewer vessels. There is also less pilferage and, hence, lower insurance rates and, finally, the assurance to the shipper that the shipment will not require any further handling until it arrives at its destination.

Among the disadvantages is the fact that each ship does not carry quite as much total volume of cargo with containers as with regular bulk stowage, because the containers themselves take space and, since they are square in shape, do not fill in all the nooks and crannies created by a ship-shaped hull form. Further, a rather substantial capital investment is needed in port facilities, such as special berths, weight-handling equipment, storage areas, and links to land transportation, all of which must be made by the ports that receive or ship via container ship if its full potential savings are to be realized.

Container ships are moderate-size merchant vessels built for speeds of greater than about 20 knots. Much use is made of small, compact, diesel power plants to provide more space for containers. Special equipment includes mooring winches to ensure accurate positioning of the ship under cranes in port and special tanks to list (tip) and trim (level) the ship to permit a symmetrical loading or unloading without excessive list or trim.

BARGE-CARRYING SHIPS

An extension of the container ship concept is the barge-carrying ship. In this concept, the container is itself a floating vessel, usually about 18 metres (60 feet) long by about 9 metres (30 feet) wide, which is loaded aboard the ship in one of two ways: either it is lifted over the stern by a high-capacity shipboard gantry crane, or the ship is partially submerged so that the barges can be floated aboard via a gate in the stern.

ROLL-ON/ROLL-OFF SHIPS

Roll-on/roll-off ships, designed for the carriage of wheeled cargo, are always distinguished by large doors in the hull and often by external ramps that fold down to allow rolling between pier and ship. Because vehicles of all kinds have some empty space—and in addition require large clearance spaces between adjacent vehicles—they constitute a low-density cargo (a high "stowage factor") that demands large hull volume. The general outline of the ship, in view of its relatively low density of cargo, is rather "boxy," with a high freeboard and a high deckhouse covering much of the ship's superstructure, to afford more parking decks. To ensure stability, fixed ballast is usually included in these

A roll-on/roll-off ship with a ramp for loading and unloading wheeled cargo.
U.S. Navy photo by MCS Seaman Kenneth R. Hendrix

ships, along with water ballast to adjust load and stability. The engineering plants are commonly twin engines of compact variety, such as geared diesel, and they are arranged so that the engine spaces are at either side of the ship, allowing valuable free space between them for vehicle passage.

DRY-BULK SHIPS

Designed for the carriage of ore, coal, grain, and the like, dry-bulk ships bear a superficial likeness to container ships since they often have no cargo handling gear and, unlike the tanker, have large cargo hatches. The absence of containers on deck is a decisive indicator that a vessel is a dry-bulk ship, but an observer may be deceived by the occasional sight of a dry-bulk ship carrying containers and other nonbulk cargo on deck. An incontrovertible indicator is the self-unloading gear, usually a large horizontal boom of open trusswork, carried by some bulk ships. On the Great Lakes of North America this gear is a near-universal feature of ships built since 1960.

GENERAL CARGO SHIP

The once-ubiquitous general cargo ship continues to be built, though in modest numbers. They are usually fitted with deck cranes, which give them an appearance distinct from the more specialized ship types.

CHAPTER 4

SHIP OPERATION

A ship is an extremely complex and expensive piece of engineering that must be operated with the greatest efficiency in order to recoup the costs of building and maintaining it. The practical aspects of running a ship and a shipping enterprise are described in this chapter.

BUSINESS ASPECTS

In the most general sense, a ship is an investment that is to be operated in such a manner that the investors' expectations with respect to returns are met. A freight rate must be obtained so that all expenses are covered, with a remainder sufficient for the returns on investment. In analysis of the economic merit of a shipping project, this rate is often referred to as the required freight rate. Actual freight rates are set by market conditions and inevitably fluctuate during the life of a ship.

THE TRAMP TRADE

The closest approximation to free-market freight rates is found in the case of the so-called tramp service offered by ships that are able to carry a variety of cargoes between a variety of ports. In many instances the services of these ships are matched with cargoes by brokers who meet face-to-face on a trading floor in an environment analogous to a stock exchange or a commodities exchange. Elements of such exchanges are present, even down to speculation on future changes in rates. For example, in times of low freight rates a broker representing cargo interests may charter a ship for a future date, all the while having no cargo in prospect but expecting to resell the contract when rates have risen.

Most of the world's tramp-ship chartering business is carried out in the Baltic Mercantile and Shipping Exchange in London, commonly known as the Baltic Exchange. Other exchanges, especially for special cargoes, are in operation. For example, a large part of the immense world oil transportation business is chartered by brokers based in a number of ports.

The four principal methods of chartering a tramp ship are voyage charter, time charter, bareboat charter, and contract charter. The voyage charter, in which a ship is chartered for a one-way voyage between specified ports, with a specified cargo at a negotiated rate of freight, is most common. The charterer agrees to provide the cargo for loading within an agreed range of dates. Once the cargo has been delivered at the port or ports of destination, the ship is free for further employment at the owner's discretion. Sometimes, however, the arrangement is for a series of consecutive voyages, generally for similar cargoes over the same route. The freight rate is expressed in terms of so much per ton of cargo delivered.

On time charter, the charterer undertakes to hire the ship for a stated period of time or for a specified round-trip voyage or, occasionally, for a stated one-way voyage, the rate of hire being expressed in terms of so much per ton deadweight per month. Whereas on a voyage charter the owner bears all the expenses of the voyage (subject to agreement about costs of loading and discharging), on time charter the charterer bears the cost of fuel and stores consumed. On bareboat charter, which is less frequently used in ordinary commercial practice, the owner of the ship delivers it up to the charterer for the agreed period without crew, stores, insurance, or any other provision, and the charterer is responsible for running the ship as if it were his own for the period of the contract.

A contract charter is usually employed when a large amount of cargo—too much for a single ship on a single voyage—is to be moved over a period of time. A typical example might be movement of a steel producer's entire supply of iron ore from mine to mill via the Great Lakes of North America. The shipowner agrees to undertake the shipment over a given period at a fixed price per ton of cargo, but not necessarily in any specified ship, although he generally uses his own ships if they are available. The question of substituted ships, however, often leads to disputes, and the terms of the contract may make special provisions for this eventuality.

THE LINER TRADE

Other shipping is done by the "liner trade"—i.e., the passage of ships between designated ports on a fixed schedule and at published rates. Liner companies are able to provide such service through the liner conference system, which was first used on the Britain-Calcutta trade in 1875. The object of the conference system is to regulate uneconomic competition. Shipping companies of different ownership and nationality that service the same range of ports form a conference agreement to regulate rates for each type of freight; in some cases the agreement also allocates a specified number of sailings to each company. Coupled with this agreement there is generally a deferred-rebate system, by which regular shippers of goods by conference vessels

ARISTOTLE ONASSIS

Aristotle Socrates Onassis was a Greek shipping magnate who developed a fleet of supertankers and freighters larger than the navies of many countries. One of the world's wealthiest individuals, he became the second husband of Jacqueline Bouvier Kennedy, the widow of U.S. Pres. John F. Kennedy, in 1968.

Onassis was born on Jan. 7, 1906, in Smyrna (now İzmir), Turkey. His family, originally wealthy tobacco dealers, lost almost everything when Smyrna, which had become a Greek city after World War I, was recaptured by the Turks in 1922. Escaping to Greece, the family sent Onassis to South America in search of a better fortune. In Buenos Aires Onassis became a night-shift switchboard operator and began a tobacco-importing business during his daytime hours. He profited from the growing popularity of imported Turkish tobacco in Argentina, and in two years earned $100,000 from commissions on tobacco sales. The Greek government tapped Onassis to negotiate a trade agreement with Argentina in 1928 and then made him consul general. His business activities expanded to include cigarette manufacturing and commodities trading. By age 25, he had made his first $1,000,000.

In 1932, during the depths of the Great Depression, Onassis bought his first six freight ships for a fraction of their actual value. He had his first oil tanker built in 1938 and acquired two more by World War II. During the war he leased his tankers and other vessels to the Allies. After the war Onassis bought 23 surplus Liberty ships from the United States, and he embarked on a program to build progressively larger oil tankers in order

Aristotle Onassis, one of the world's great shipping magnates. Ron Galella/WireImage/Getty Images

to transport economically the world's supply of petroleum. He initiated the construction of supertankers, in 1954 alone commissioning 17 such vessels. During the Arab-Israeli wars in 1956 and 1967, his tankers reaped immense profits transporting oil from the Middle East via the Cape of Good Hope route after the Suez Canal had been closed.

In 1953 Onassis purchased a controlling interest in the Société des Bains de Mer, which owned the casino, hotels, and other real estate in the resort of Monte Carlo. From 1957 to 1974 he also owned and operated Olympic Airways, the Greek national airlines, by concession from the Greek government. His lavish yacht *Christina*, named for his daughter, served for many years as his permanent residence.

Onassis's first marriage, in 1946, was to Athina Livanos, a daughter of the shipping magnate Stavros Livanos; it ended in divorce in 1960. He was long intimately associated with the opera diva Maria Callas, but in 1968 he abruptly married Jacqueline Kennedy, who was more than 20 years his junior. The two divided their time between New York, Paris, and Onassis's private island resort of Skorpios, in the Ionian Sea. Onassis died in the Paris suburb of Neuilly-sur-Seine on March 15, 1975.

receive a rebate of a percentage of the tariff freight rate, payable after a period of proven loyalty, provided they use conference vessels exclusively.

The shipping conference system has sometimes come under attack as tending to create a monopoly and to restrain competition against the public interest. It is, however, generally agreed that evidence is in favour of this system: it has been concluded that no realistically possible combination of shipping companies can force unreasonable rates and that shipping companies that provide regular sailings with good ships and maintain staffs and organizations in ports to handle and dispatch

cargoes—irrespective of whether trade is good or bad—
are entitled to some protection against the casual vessel
that picks up an occasional cargo at cut rates. Advocates
agree that through the system the shipper can rely on a
well-managed service, running vessels that will carry any
desired quantities of goods at predetermined rates.

THE CAPTIVE FLEET

A third scheme of organization is the captive fleet, a shipping company that is a subsidiary of a larger entity that
moves its own cargo in a continuous stream. Prominent
examples are the fleets owned by many major petroleum
companies to bring crude oil to their refineries and to
distribute their products from refinery to distribution
centres.

INTERNATIONAL CONVENTIONS

Ships historically made untrammeled use of the vast ocean
surface. The necessity of coming into port gave shore
authorities the opportunity to exact certain payments,
but, until regulation began to appear in the middle of the
19th century, owners and captains were free to do as they
pleased in building and operating their ships. As maritime
nations began to realize that accidents at sea were prevent-
able by adherence to rules for the building and operation
of ships, a body of regulations began to develop under the
powers of individual states to make laws for their own citizens (and for others within controlled waters). However,
given that ships of all nations were free to use the ocean,
diversity of rules was a serious problem, with maritime
trade readily falling into the hands of the ships that obeyed
the least onerous rules.

The practice of enforced observance of local regulations continues, but since the late 19th century a series of agreements among maritime states has brought near-uniformity to regulations governing ship operation and aspects of ship design and equipage that bear on safety. Nearly all the world's maritime states, for example, have adopted the International Regulations for Preventing Collisions at Sea (known as COLREGS). These were originally based on British rules formulated in 1862 and made internationally effective after a series of international meetings culminating in a conference at Washington, D.C., in 1889. The rules specify in great detail how ships must navigate in respect of each other, what lights must be shown, and what signals must be given in accordance with circumstances. Any infringement of this international code of conduct is accepted in all maritime courts

(Right) *Efthimios Mitropoulos, secretary-general of the International Maritime Organization, being greeted by Najib Razak* (left), *deputy prime minister and minister of defense of Malaysia.* Teh Eng Koon/AFP/Getty Images

of law as prima facie evidence of liability in case of collision. Similarly, the internationally accepted requirements for the protection and safety of life at sea, as far as the ship and its equipment are concerned, are embodied in the International Convention for Safety of Life at Sea (known as SOLAS). The sinking of the liner *Titanic* in 1912 gave rise to a general desire to raise the standards of safety of life at sea. Although a convention was drawn up in 1914 requiring certain minimum standards for passenger ships, it did not become fully operative because of the outbreak of World War I.

The advent of the United Nations after World War II brought into being a permanent international body, the International Maritime Organization (IMO), an arm of the UN whose purpose is to produce and modify international conventions in three categories: safety, prevention of pollution, and liability and compensation following accidents. The IMO has produced a regulatory literature too extensive to detail here, but four conventions that have the greatest bearing on ship operation can be mentioned. The International Convention on Load Lines of 1966 emerged from the British Merchant Shipping Act of 1875, which provided what was known as the Plimsoll load line on the ship's side, indicating the maximum depth to which a ship could legally be loaded. In order to protect the competitive position of British ships, the Merchant Shipping Act of 1890 required all foreign ships leaving British ports to comply with the load-line regulations. This led to the adoption of load-line rules by most maritime countries, and the International Load Line Convention of 1930 was ratified by 54 nations. The new convention of 1966 came into force in July 1968 and allowed for a smaller freeboard (vertical distance between the water and the deck) for large ships while calling for more stringent protection of openings in decks and superstructures. The Convention on International Regulations for Preventing Collisions at Sea and the International Convention for the Safety of Life at Sea were drawn up in 1972 and 1974, respectively. In 1973 and 1978 the International Convention for the Prevention of Pollution from Ships (MARPOL) came up with regulations that cover internal arrangements of tankers in order to minimize oil spills following hull ruptures.

IMO regulations do not go into effect until they have been ratified by a sufficient number of maritime states. In turn, they are not enforced by the regulatory arm of a maritime state until they have also become the law of that land. In the United States, for example, they must become federal law by the usual passage through Congress and the Executive. They are thereafter found in the Code of Federal Regulations and are enforced by the United States Coast Guard within U.S. waters. The enforcement functions of the U.S. Coast Guard are largely focused in a Certificate of Inspection that is required for commercial shipping under its jurisdiction. The owner of a vessel required to have this certificate must submit certain construction plans and other data for approval during the design and building stages. Inspectors from the Coast Guard may visit the vessel while it is under construction. The certificate, required before operation of the ship, is posted aboard as tangible proof that federal law has been complied with. The certificate also lists safety equipment that must be carried and specifies the minimum crew that must be employed.

SHIP CLASSIFICATION

In most maritime states, nongovernmental regulatory bodies are empowered to carry out such legally mandated actions as assigning load lines and to publish rules for ship design that must be complied with for insurability.

However, since their functions are to establish an insurability class for new ships whose owners opt for this service and to survey the ships periodically for continued compliance over their lifetime, they are more accurately described as classification societies.

The leading classification society, operating in almost every country in the world, is Lloyd's Register of Shipping, which began its work long before any national legislation existed for the performance of its purposes. The history of Lloyd's Register of Shipping can be traced back to 1760. The society was reconstituted in 1834 and again in 1914. Lloyd's operates in most maritime countries, often in cooperation with classification societies established by other nations. These include the American Bureau of Shipping, originally established in 1867 and resuscitated as a result of the large volume of merchant ships built in the United States during World Wars I and II; the Bureau Veritas, which was founded in Antwerp (Belg.) in 1828 but moved its headquarters to Paris in 1832; the Norske Veritas, established in Norway in 1894; Germanischer Lloyd, founded in Germany in 1867; and Registro Italiano Navale, founded in Italy in 1861.

CREWING

As powered ships developed in the 19th century, their crews evolved into three distinct groups: (1) the deck department, which steered, kept lookout, handled lines in docking and undocking, and performed at-sea maintenance on the hull and nonmachinery components, (2) the engine department, which operated machinery and performed at-sea maintenance, and (3) the stewards department, which did the work of a hotel staff for the crew and passengers. The total number of crew varied widely with the function of the ship and with changes in technology. For example, an early 20th-century transatlantic liner might carry 500 stewards, 300 crew members in its engine department (most of them occupied in hand-firing the boilers), and 70 crew in its deck department. The later adoption of oil fuel and also of the diesel engine allowed a drastic cut in the engineering department. Still later, such devices as autopilots for steering and automatic constant-tension mooring winches allowed reductions in the deck department. Meanwhile, the need for stewards on passenger ships has remained high: a cruise ship will still carry a stewards department of several hundred.

In 1960 a steam-powered cargo ship (operating under the U.S. flag) might carry a crew of 45, comprising 20 deck (6 licensed officers), 16 engineering (6 licensed officers), 8 stewards, and 1 radio officer. By 1990 the crew for a similar ship, which was likely to be diesel-powered, might number 21—all three departments having been shrunk by technological advances that reduced not only labour but also the need for watch-standing, especially in the engine room, where automatic control and monitoring has obviated the need for constant attendance on machinery.

As of 1990 U.S. law required distinct deck and engine departments and sufficient personnel for three watches a day—requirements difficult to meet with a crew of less than 20. However, experiments in fleets of other maritime nations show that current technology allows a crew to number as few as 10. In order to attain such minimal crewing, the traditional distinction between engine and deck departments must be removed in favour of persons trained as "ship operators." With machinery automated to the extent that it can be monitored and controlled from the ship's wheelhouse—and with much of the maintenance done by special roving teams that can come by air from a distant home base—crews on the order of 10 in number may become generally accepted.

MAINTENANCE

In general, ships have a maintenance requirement similar to that of large buildings. However, they also have unique maintenance requirements, and these are usually of such magnitude that they obscure the similarities to shore maintenance.

REPAIRING MARINE DAMAGE

The largest and most obvious area unique to ship maintenance is repairing the ravages of the marine environment. In particular the salts of the sea, which are carried by spray to all exterior surfaces, are corrosive to common shipbuilding steels. Corrosion-resistant materials are too expensive for general use, so that the maintenance of a protective coating is the only alternative to control rusting. Cleaning of deteriorated surfaces and their repainting has therefore been the largest maintenance task for most 20th-century ships. The rapid development of coatings that protect steel surfaces better by adhering better and being themselves more resistant to sea salts has been a major factor in allowing reduction of crew size.

Tankers are often required to clean the interiors of their cargo tanks, a task that is usually done with heated seawater. Protection of their surfaces from the corrosive water by conventional paints is ineffective, and ships that have no better protection than that are usually short-lived because of the consequent wastage of their structure. Coatings that may be described generically as "plastics" are much more effective than paints but are also much more expensive; nevertheless, the expense is often justified by the extended life of the ship they provide.

Removal of marine growths—most commonly the crustacean familiarly known (and cursed) as the barnacle—from underwater surfaces is a major maintenance task that has always plagued ocean shipping. The 20th century has seen the development of increasingly effective antifouling coatings whose expense has to be balanced by reduced maintenance costs and by the fuel savings that result from smoother surfaces. Some of the most effective coatings are forbidden, at least in some areas, because of their threat to the marine environment.

MAINTAINING MACHINERY

The maintenance to be expected with a ship's propulsion machinery depends on the type of machinery in question. For a steam turbine propulsion plant, the major maintenance items are likely to be those associated with the

A technician checking a gas-turbine engine on a U.S. Navy destroyer. U.S. Navy photo by PH3c Jordon R. Beesley

boilers. Boiler tubes are subject to fouling on both the water side and the hot gas side and may require periodic cleaning. Also, the refractory material ("firebrick") used in a boiler furnace may require occasional renewal. A boiler, being a fired pressure vessel, is under legal stricture to have periodic safety inspections, which require removal from service and opening.

In a diesel propulsion plant, the engine itself is likely to be the main focus of maintenance work. The principal causes are high temperature in the engine cylinders and the unavoidable wear that takes place at points of sliding contact, such as piston ring against cylinder wall. The corrosive combustion products of low-quality fuels may also exacerbate matters. Given that the propulsion engine of a long-voyage commercial ship may operate at its rated power for 6,000 to 7,000 hours per year, frequent replacement of wearing parts (annually in some cases) is inevitable.

CARGO HANDLING

A commercial ship is usually a link in a "trade route" between distant points. Goods flowing in the route must be transferred to and from the sea link; they must also be given care while aboard the ship, and in turn they must not be a hazard to the ship and its crew.

SHIP-SHORE TRANSFER

Ancient cargo handling consisted almost exclusively of manually carrying cargo in single man-loads. For example, grain would be packed into sacks, each of a size that a man could carry on or off the ship on his shoulders. During the many centuries of dominance by sailing vessels, this process might be supplemented by hoisting with the ship's running rigging. A line reeved through a block on the end of a yard might be led to a capstan by which a group of men might develop the force needed to lift an object far heavier than a single man-load.

Steam propulsion brought the steam winch and rigging that was intended solely for lifting cargo. The near-universal practice as it developed into the 20th century was to fit at least one pair of booms to serve each cargo hatchway, with each boom supported by rigging from a "king post," a short, stout mast whose sole function was boom support. Winches were mounted at the base of the king post. In action, the head of one boom would be rigged in fixed position over the hatchway; the head of the other would be rigged over the cargo-handling space on the pier alongside. A single lifting hook would be used, but a line would lead from the hook to each of the two boom-heads ("married falls") and thence each to its individual winch. By cooperative tensioning and slackening of the two lines, the winch operators could cause the hook to move vertically directly beneath either boom-head or horizontally between them. Cargo was thereby moved between cargo hold and pier with no gear movement save that of the hook and its two supporting lines. This scheme is known as burtoning.

Burtoning was gradually replaced by systems better adapted to special cargoes. It remained in favour only for handling very heavy objects, so that the few ships that were built during the late 20th century for this type of cargo were usually fitted with at least one set of massive burtoning gear. The first cargo to require a unique handling system was petroleum. When first carried by sea, petroleum products were packaged in barrels that were handled in the traditional way, but the great volume to be moved quickly soon made this method of packaging and handling woefully inadequate. Since the late 19th century crude oil and its many products have been transported in bulk—i.e., without packaging. The hulls of tankers are subdivided into a number of cells, or tanks, into which the liquid cargo is pumped through hoses by pumps mounted on the shore. Unloading is effected in the reverse manner by pumps mounted within the ship. Usually the only external cargo-handling gear is a pair of cranes or boom-post winch sets (one for each side of the ship) for handling the rather massive hoses that connect the ship to the shore facility.

The handling of many other commodities is more economical if done without packaging and with at least some of the continuous-flow features of pumping. For example, the loading of "dry bulk" commodities such as coal, ore, and grain is nearly always done from special shore facilities that pour them from a high elevation directly into the cargo holds of the ship. Although the ship may be designed

Sacks of sugar being loaded by conveyor into the hold of a cargo ship. Bloomberg via Getty Images

for the commodity, almost any cargo-carrying ship except the tanker can accept dry-bulk cargoes in this fashion.

Discharging dry bulk is another matter. It can be lifted from the holds by grab buckets, but conventional burtoning gear is ill-suited for the operation of these devices. For this reason cargo terminals that receive bulk cargo are often equipped with unloading cranes that are especially suited for grab-bucket operation or with vacuum hoses for moving low-density cargo such as grain. Special-purpose dry-bulk ships may therefore be without onboard cargo handling gear. Examples are the ships built before 1970 to carry iron ore on the Great Lakes of North America.

Since 1970 all such ships built for Great Lakes service have been fitted with their own unloading gear, and their example has been followed by many oceangoing carriers of dry bulk. The handling gear usually consists of a series of three conveyor belts. The first runs under the cargo holds, whence it may receive the cargo through hopper doors in the bottom. The second belt receives the cargo from the first and carries it to the main deck level of the hull. There it discharges to the belt that carries the cargo to the end of a discharge boom, whence the cargo is dumped onto the receiving ground ashore. The discharge boom can be slewed and elevated to reach the appropriate discharge point. A continuously acting onboard discharge system of this type can attain much higher discharge rates than grab buckets, and it avoids the damage to hull surfaces that is inevitable in bucket operation. Further, it gives a ship the flexibility to serve points that are not fitted with unloading gear.

The economic burden of handling nonbulk (or "break-bulk") cargoes in small batches is less evident than with cargoes that can be pumped, poured, or conveyed, but it was making itself very evident as early as the 1950s. The revenue lost from keeping a ship in port while it was slowly—and at high labour cost—loaded or unloaded was one factor; another was the inherent labour-intensiveness of moving cargo horizontally in order to reach the hoisting gear and then loading and unloading rail cars and trucks at pierside. By 1960 these factors had led to the introduction of standardized steel or aluminum containers— 2.4 × 2.4 × 12 metres (8 × 8 × 40 feet) in the most common size—into which almost any nonbulk commodity could be stowed. The primary advantages in containerized shipping are the radical reduction in the number of cargo pieces to be handled and the high degree of protection the containers provide to the cargo items. Further advantages come from designing ships specifically for carriage of containers, shoreside terminals for their rapid transfer, and land vehicles for their carriage. These additional steps were put into place quite rapidly after the container concept was introduced.

The essential feature of container ships is a width of hatchway that allows the containers to be handled solely by vertical lifting and lowering. This feature is usually supplemented by vertical guide rails that divide the cargo holds into cells that are sized precisely to hold stacks of containers. Labour within the hold is thereby reduced to insignificance. A consequence of great value is the freedom from "dunnage," the packing and bracing necessary to immobilize the usual odd-sized nonbulk cargoes. The highway trailers and railcars that form the land part of the trade route are similarly designed to fit the container, thereby making the shoreside handling rapid and virtually free of hands-on labour. Cranes and lifting gear designed for handling the standard-size containers are the third part of the rapid and economical ship/shore transfer. Cranes best-suited to this service are usually too massive for shipboard mounting and, hence, are part of the terminal. Typical container ships are therefore not fitted with cargo handling gear .

In loading or unloading a barge-carrying ship, no shore terminal or any special shore vehicle is required, since delivery to or from the ship is by water. Where the seaport is at the mouth of an extensive river system, the ultimate terminus can be at a great distance from the ship. Points not adjacent to a navigable waterway can be served as well, although an extra step of transfer to or from a land link is required.

When the cargo has wheels—e.g., automobiles, trucks, and railway cars—the most satisfactory cargo handling method is simply to roll it on and off. Vehicle ferries have been familiar in many waters for many centuries, and the growth since about 1960 of an extensive international trade in motor vehicles has led to an extension of the ferry principle into roll-on/roll-off ships, which carry automobiles strictly as cargo yet load and unload them by driving them on their own wheels. Ships built for "ro-ro" traffic are fitted with doors in the hull (most often at the ends), internal ramps and elevators for deck-to-deck transfers, and external ramps to join the hull doors to the pier. Often the main or only door is in the stern, facing directly aft and fitted with a massive folding ramp exterior to the hull. The ramp is often equipped for slewing—i.e., rotating so that it can be landed on a pier alongside the ship.

Although many types of cargo are handled by gear that is designed for a particular type, general-purpose equipment retains a niche. However, the traditional burtoning gear has almost disappeared among new buildings in favour of cranes that are adapted from shoreside lifting machinery. This alternative is usually less costly to build and maintain, and it requires less labour in operation.

HANDLING ABOARD SHIP

Many types of cargo require protection from hazards peculiar to a sea passage and from deterioration that may occur from the more general exigencies of transportation. A prominent example of the latter problem is any food product that must be refrigerated during its entire transit from producer to consumer. Ships built with insulated and refrigerated cargo holds are essential to moving such products by sea, though an alternative is transport in insulated and refrigerated containers. In the latter case, the container ship must be fitted with a means of supplying the necessary electric power to the containers.

Cargo carried belowdecks is usually safe from the corrosiveness of seawater, but ship motion from wave action is pervasive. Any nonbulk cargo must be securely fastened in place. Guide rails for containers, usually fitted in container ships, automatically secure any below-deck containers against movement, thereby precluding the labour-intensive task of preparing the cargo to withstand ship motion.

Many liquid cargoes need to be heated because they may otherwise require excessive energy to pump. Some, such as sulfur and asphalt, are liquid, and hence pumpable, only when they are kept at high temperature. Foodstuffs may require refrigeration, but other cold products fall in a cryogenic temperature range that is beyond the capability of shipboard equipment. An example is liquefied natural gas. Ships that carry this product must have cargo tanks that are so heavily insulated that only a small fraction of the cargo is lost to evaporation during a normal voyage.

Protecting cargo while it is aboard ship is obviously crucial, but in many ways cargoes can be a hazard to ship, crew, and public. Protection against hazardous cargo is therefore also an essential element of cargo handling. Even the most benign cargoes may be a danger to the ship. Grain, for example, can swell from wetting and so produce dangerous pressure against the cargo hold structure. Also, it can flow like any granular product and so may shift to the low side of a ship, exacerbating a heeling angle. Petroleum products are highly flammable and, moreover, may give rise to explosive vapour-air mixtures within a cargo tank. An empty petroleum tank is especially dangerous, since remnants of cargo clinging to the tank have a large surface area in contact with air. The typical safeguard is to displace the air within the tanks by an inert gas—usually air that is depleted of oxygen by having passed through the combustion process in the ship's propulsion machinery.

The oil spill that may follow a collision or grounding of a tanker is an often-disastrous feature of the petroleum age. Tankers traditionally are not fitted with double bottoms, because the breaching of a tank that is already filled with liquid is not likely to lead to the sinking of the ship. However, the most serious oil spills have followed from bottom damage in grounding accidents, and they would not have happened if an unbreached inner bottom had maintained tank integrity. The current regulatory trend is toward legal requirement of double bottoms in at least the large crude-oil carriers that are the most likely source of devastating spills.

The interiors of oil cargo tanks must be washed occasionally, especially when the ship is preparing to carry a different product on its next voyage. The washings, if discharged indiscriminately, are noxious to the marine environment, and hence marine laws require that the oil be separated and held aboard for discharge into a safe receiving facility in port.

Some bulk cargoes can be corrosive to the structure of the cargo tank or hold, or they may undergo spontaneous reactions that can lead to combustion or—in extreme cases—to explosions. Some substances react violently with water or with other materials that may inadvertently be stowed in the same hold. Given the immense number and variety of substances moving in commerce, their many hazards, and the many possible ways of packaging them, there must also be a large and complex body of regulations governing their movement. For shipment by water, the many regulations are based on the Dangerous Goods Code of the International Maritime Organization, and they are implemented by the various national laws that are based on this code.

CHAPTER 5

SHIP DESIGN

The design of ships employs many technologies and branches of engineering that also are found ashore, but the imperatives of effective and safe operation at sea require oversight from a unique discipline. That discipline is properly called marine engineering, but the term *naval architecture* is familiarly used in the same sense. In this chapter the latter term is used to denote the hydrostatic and aesthetic aspects of marine engineering.

The measurements of ships are given in terms of length, breadth, and depth. The length between perpendiculars is the distance on the summer (maximum) load waterline, from the forward side of the stem at the extreme forward part of the vessel to the after side of the rudder post at the extreme rear, or to the centre of the rudder stock, if there is no rudder post. The beam is the greatest breadth of the ship. The depth is measured at the middle of the length, from the top of the keel to the top of the deck beam at the side of the uppermost continuous deck. Draft is measured from the keel to the waterline, while freeboard is measured from the waterline to the deck edge.

THE NAVAL ARCHITECT

A naval architect asked to design a ship may receive his instructions in a form ranging from such simple requirements as "an oil tanker to carry 100,000 tons deadweight at 15 knots" to a fully detailed specification of precisely planned requirements. He is usually required to prepare a design for a vessel that must carry a certain weight of cargo (or number of passengers) at a specified speed with particular reference to trade requirements; high-density cargoes, such as machinery, require little hold capacity, while the reverse is true for low-density cargoes, such as grain.

Deadweight is defined as weight of cargo plus fuel and consumable stores, and lightweight as the weight of the hull, including machinery and equipment. The designer must choose dimensions such that the displacement of the vessel is equal to the sum of the deadweight and the lightweight tonnages. The fineness of the hull must be appropriate to the speed. The draft—which is governed by freeboard rules—enables the depth to be determined to a first approximation.

After selecting tentative values of length, breadth, depth, draft, and displacement, the designer must achieve a weight balance. He must also select a moment balance because centres of gravity in both longitudinal and vertical directions must provide satisfactory trim and stability. Additionally, he must estimate the shaft horse-power required for the specified speed; this determines the weight of machinery. The strength of the hull must be adequate for the service intended; detailed scantlings (frame dimensions and plate thicknesses) can be obtained from the rules of the classification society. These scant-lings determine the requisite weight of hull steel.

The vessel should possess satisfactory steering characteristics and freedom from troublesome vibration and should comply with the many varied requirements of international regulations. Possessing an attractive appearance, the ship should have the minimum net register tonnage, the factor on which harbour and other dues are based. (The gross tonnage represents the volume of all closed-in spaces above the inner bottom. The net tonnage is the gross tonnage minus certain deductible spaces that do not produce revenue. Net tonnage can therefore be regarded as a measure of the earning capacity of the ship, hence its use as a basis for harbour and docking charges.) Passenger vessels must satisfy a standard of bulkhead subdivision that will ensure adequate stability under specified conditions if the hull is pierced accidentally, as through collision.

Compromise plays a considerable part in producing a satisfactory design. A naval architect must be a master of approximations. If the required design closely resembles that of a ship already built for which full information is available, the designer can calculate the effects of differences between this ship and the projected ship. If, however, this information is not available, he must first produce coefficients based upon experience and, after refining them, check the results by calculation.

HYDROSTATICS

The basis of naval architecture is found in Archimedes' principle, which states that the weight of a statically floating body must equal the weight of the volume of water that it displaces. This law of buoyancy determines not only the draft at which a vessel will float but also the angles that it will assume when in equilibrium with the water.

A ship may be designed to carry a specified weight of cargo, plus such necessary supplies as fuel, lubricating oil, crew, and the crew's life support. To this deadweight must be added the weight of the ship's structure, propulsion machinery, hull engineering (nonpropulsive machinery), and outfit (fixed items having to do with crew life support).

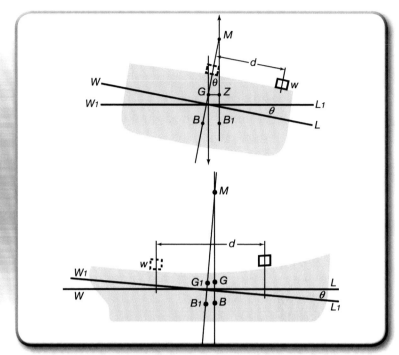

Static stability of a ship. (Top) Transverse section of a ship floating at heel angle Θ with load w shfited away from centre. (Bottom) Longitudinal section of a ship floating at waterline WL, showing change to trim angle Θ with load w shifted toward the stern.

These categories of weight are known collectively as light-ship weight. The sum of deadweight and lightship weight is displacement—that is, the weight that must be equaled by the weight of displaced water if the ship is to float. Of course, the volume of water displaced by a ship is a function of the size of that ship, but in turn the weight of water that is to be matched by displacement is also a function of the ship's size. The early stages of ship design, therefore, are a struggle to predict the size of the ship that the sum of all weights will require. The naval architect's resources include experience-based formulas that provide approximate values for making such predictions. Subsequent refinements usually produce accurate predictions of the ship's draft—that is, the depth of water in which the finished ship will float.

In some cases a ship may be intended for cargo of such a high stowage factor (i.e., volume per weight unit) that providing for the required internal volume is more of a problem than providing for a specific deadweight. Nevertheless, the problem of designing for a displacement that matches the weight of the ship is essentially the same.

STATIC STABILITY

Accurately predicting a ship's draft is a necessary result of correctly applied hydrostatic principles but is far from sufficient. If the many items of weight on a ship are not distributed with considerable precision, the ship will float at unwanted angles of heel (sideways inclination) and trim (endwise inclination). Nonzero trim angles may lift the tips of propeller blades above the surface, or they may increase the possibility that the bow will slam into waves during heavy weather. Nonzero heel angles (which tend to be much greater than trim angles) may make all human activity aboard difficult; moreover, they are dangerous because they reduce the margin against capsizing. In general, the avoidance of such inclinations requires an extension of Archimedes' principle to the first moments of weights and volumes: the collective first moment of all weights must equal the first weight moment of the water displaced.

A figure depicting the static stability of a ship shows the cross section of a ship that is floating at heel angle θ, caused by the placement of a weight (w) a certain distance (d) from the centre line. At this angle, the upsetting moment, calculated as $w \times d \times \cos \theta$, is equaled by the righting moment $Q \times GZ$, (Q is the symbol for displacement, and GZ is the distance from the centre of gravity [G] to the centre of buoyancy [Z]). Under these conditions, the ship is said to be in static equilibrium. If w is removed, the upsetting moment will become zero, and the righting moment will return the ship to its upright position. The ship is therefore judged to be stable. The moment will act in the stable direction only as long as the point M (the "metacentre," the point where the buoyant force intersects the midplane) is above G (the centre of gravity of the ship and its contents). If M is below G, the forces of weight and buoyancy will tend to increase the angle of heel, and the equilibrium will be unstable. The distance from G to M, taken to be positive if M is above G, is called the transverse metacentric height.

A value for metacentric height is usually found only for the zero heel condition; hence, it is an accurate measure of stability only for small disturbances—for example, ones that cause heeling of no more than about 10°. For larger angles, the "righting arm," $G\,Z$, is used to measure stability. In any stability analysis, the value of $G\,Z$ is plotted over the entire range of heel angles for which it is positive, or restoring. The resultant curve of statical stability shows thereby the angle beyond which the ship cannot return to upright and the angle at which the restoring moment is at a maximum. The area of the curve between its origin and any specified angle is proportional to the energy required to heel the ship to that angle.

DYNAMIC STABILITY

The capsizing of large ships that have not suffered flooding from hull damage is virtually unheard of, but it remains a serious hazard to smaller vessels that can experience large upsetting moments under normal operating conditions. A prominent example is a fishing vessel attempting to lift a laden net over the side while already being rolled by heavy seas. In any case, a capsizing is likely to be a dynamic event rather than a static one—a consequence, for example, of the impact from a wind gust. Such an input is properly measured in terms of capsizing energy, and hence the ability of a ship to resist capsizing is measured by the energy required to rotate it to a point of vanishing stability. As noted, the resisting energy is indicated by the area enclosed by the statical stability curve; standards by which the stability of ships are judged are therefore usually based on this area. Because of the great variability of ship sizes, types, and areas of service, safety standards of all kinds, managed by the International Maritime Organization (IMO), are complex.

DAMAGE BUOYANCY AND STABILITY

Building a ship that can be neither sunk nor capsized is beyond practicality, but a ship can be designed to survive moderate damage and, if sinking is inevitable, to sink slowly and without capsizing in order to maximize the survival chances of the people aboard.

The most likely cause of sinking would be a breaching of the hull envelope by collision. The consequences of the resulting flooding are minimized by subdividing of the hull into compartments by watertight bulkheads. The extent to which such bulkheads are fitted is determined by IMO standards that are based on the size and type of ship. At a minimum, ships that must have a high probability of surviving a collision (e.g., passenger ships) are built to the "one-compartment" standard, meaning that at least one compartment bounded by watertight bulkheads must be floodable without sinking the ship. A two-compartment standard is common for larger passenger-carrying ships—a measure that presumably protects the ship against a collision at the boundary between two compartments. The *Titanic*, the victim of the most famous sinking in the North Atlantic, was built to the two-compartment standard, but its collision with an iceberg just before midnight on April 14, 1912, ripped open at least five compartments. The *Titanic* could not survive such damage, but its many watertight bulkheads did retard the flooding so that the ship required two hours and forty minutes to sink.

To build a passenger ship that would survive all possible floodings is impractical, since the required fine subdivision would preclude effective use of the interior space. On the other hand, a ship carrying only liquid cargo can be subdivided quite finely, since most of its interior space is tankage. Such ships are at hazard from groundings and explosions, but their sinking from collisions is very rare.

In contrast to the *Titanic*, the *Lusitania*, a passenger liner of similar size and type, sank within a period of 20 minutes after being hit by two torpedoes on May 7, 1915. Its

Front page of the New York Times *detailing the sinking of the* Lusitania. MPI/Archive Photos/Getty Images

THE TITANIC

When the British passenger liner *Titanic* left Southampton, Eng., on April 10, 1912, for its maiden voyage to New York, it was one of the largest and most luxurious ships in the world. It had a gross registered tonnage (i.e., carrying capacity) of 46,329 tons, and when fully laden the ship displaced 66,000 tons. The ship was 269 metres (882.5 feet) long and 28.2 metres (92.5 feet) wide at its widest point. It had been designed and built by William Pirrie's Belfast firm Harland and Wolff to service the highly competitive Atlantic Ferry route. It had a double-bottomed hull divided into 16 compartments that were presumed to be watertight. Because four of these could be flooded without endangering the liner's buoyancy, the *Titanic* was considered unsinkable.

Shortly before midnight on April 14, the ship collided with an iceberg about 640 km (400 miles) south of Newfoundland, and at least five of its watertight compartments toward the bow were ruptured. The first four of these five compartments filled with water, which pulled down the bow of the ship. The *Titanic*'s compartments were not capped at the top, so water from the ruptured forward compartments filled each succeeding compartment aft as the ship's incline brought the bow below the waterline. The ship sank at 2:20 AM April 15. The *Titanic* had only 1,178 lifeboat spaces for the 2,224 persons aboard, and many of the lifeboats were lowered into the water only partly filled with passengers, thus leaving many people stranded on the sinking ship. As a result, about 1,500 people died.

Inquiries held in the United States and Great Britain alleged that the Leyland liner *Californian*, which was less than 32 km (20 miles) away all night, could have aided the stricken vessel had its radio operator been on duty and thereby received the *Titanic*'s distress signals. Only the arrival of the Cunard liner *Carpathia* 1 hour and 20 minutes after the *Titanic* went down prevented further loss of life in the icy waters.

Many of those who perished on the ship came from prominent American, British, and European families. Among the dead were the noted British journalist William Thomas Stead and heirs to the Straus and Astor fortunes. The glamour associated with the ship, its maiden voyage, and its notable passengers magnified the tragedy of its sinking in the popular mind. Legends arose almost immediately around the night's events, those who had died, and those who had survived.

Heroes and heroines, such as American Molly Brown, were identified and celebrated by the press.

As a result of the disaster, the first International Convention for Safety of Life at Sea was called in London in 1913. The convention drew up rules requiring that every ship have lifeboat space for each person embarked; that lifeboat drills be held during each voyage; and, because the *Californian* had not heard the distress signals of the *Titanic*, that ships maintain a 24-hour radio watch. The International Ice Patrol also was established to warn ships of icebergs in the North Atlantic shipping lanes.

On Sept. 1, 1985, the wreck of the *Titanic* was found lying upright in two pieces on the ocean floor at a depth of about 4,000 metres (13,000 feet). The ship, located at about 41°46' N 50°14' W, was subsequently explored several times by manned and unmanned submersibles under the direction of American and French scientists. The expeditions found no sign of the long gash previously thought to have been ripped in the ship's hull by the iceberg. The scientists posited instead that the collision's impact had produced a series of thin gashes as well as brittle fracturing and separation of seams in the adjacent hull plates, thus allowing water to flood in and sink the ship. In subsequent years marine salvagers raised small artifacts from the wreckage as well as pieces of the ship itself, including a large section of the hull. Examination of these parts—as well as paperwork in the builder's archives—led to speculation that low-quality steel or weak rivets may have contributed to the *Titanic*'s sinking.

fault lay not in insufficient subdivision but in lack of damage stability. Longitudinal bulkheads in the vicinity of the torpedo hits limited the flooding to one side, causing the ship to heel quickly to the point where normal hull openings were submerged. As a consequence of this disaster, commercial ships are now forbidden from having internal structures that impede flooding across the hull. An exception to this regulation is the tanker, whose subdivision is fine enough that flooding of several side tanks is insufficient to capsize the ship.

One important hazard in considering damage stability is the "free surface effect." Water that is unconfined—as flooding water that enters a damaged hull is likely to be—runs to the lowest reachable point, thus exacerbating the heel that caused the low point. Such a hazard is difficult to avoid in ships that must have interior spaces uninterrupted by bulkheads. Ferries, which usually require vehicle decks extending throughout their interiors, are an example.

SHIP HYDRODYNAMICS

Up to now the focus of this chapter has been on the stability of a ship at rest. This section deals with hydrodynamics, the stability of a ship in motion.

DESIGN OF THE HULL

The shape of a ship hull is determined by many competing influences. For ease of construction, it should be a rectangular box; for adequate transverse stability, it must be wide; for adequate strength as a beam being bent in a longitudinal plane, it must be deep. All these factors influence the shape of a hull, but often the primary factor is the dynamic interaction of the hull with the water. The interactions that govern the resistance of the hull to steady forward motion—a resistance that determines the choice of propulsive power—usually demand the greatest attention from the naval architect.

Resistance to steady forward motion has four components: (1) friction between the water and the hull surfaces, (2) energy expended in creating the wave system caused by the hull, (3) energy put into eddies shed by the hull and its

The hull of a ship. Digital Vision/Thinkstock

appendages (e.g., the rudder), and (4) resistance by the air to above-water parts of the ship.

Frictional resistance is proportional to the product of water density, area of contact with the water, square of water speed relative to the ship, and a friction coefficient. This resistance can be minimized by reducing the area of a hull's wetted surface, but usually very little can be accomplished in the face of many other demands on hull size and shape. A smooth surface is an obvious factor in reducing friction, but a surface that is smoother than ordinary painted steel has a benefit that is trivial compared to its cost. The friction coefficient is largely a function of the Reynolds number (the product of water density times ship speed times ship length, divided by water viscosity); it is not controllable by a designer since water density and viscosity are beyond control and ship length and speed are almost inevitably dictated by other considerations. The friction coefficient was the subject of intense research, especially during the first half of the 20th century, but since that time most ship designers have employed values standardized by the International Towing Tank Conference.

Wave-making and eddy-making resistance components are often lumped into a single "residuary resistance," especially when resistance measurements are extrapolated from model testing. Wave making is usually by far the larger component of residuary resistance; it is therefore given more attention in research and in the designing of a hull. Indeed, wave making increases so rapidly as ship speed increases that it eventually requires more power to overcome than is practicable to build into a ship. For a ship of conventional type, it is virtually impossible to operate at a speed-to-length ratio (speed in nautical miles per hour, divided by the square root of the waterline length in feet) higher than approximately 1.3. Beyond that realm even a trivial increase in speed requires a virtually infinite increase in power in order to fulfill the energy demand of the wave system. Small craft can escape this limitation by planing, but the amount of power required for the transition to a planing mode is beyond practicality for conventional ships.

A significant feature of waves generated by the passage of a ship is that they travel at the same speed as the ship and that their speed (like that of surface waves in general) is proportional to the square root of their length. In consequence, when a ship is running at a speed-to-length ratio of 1.0, its waterline length is the same as the crest-to-crest length of its wave pattern, in effect putting it into a hole of its own making. As more power is applied, the hole becomes deeper until any further increase in speed simply poses the impossible task of climbing out of the hole.

Another significant feature of ship-generated waves is their origin at different parts of the hull. A bow wave and a stern wave are always present, and, if the fore and after parts of the hull fair into a straight mid-body with distinct shoulders, then these shoulders also will produce waves. It may well happen that the crests of waves from one source will coincide with the troughs of another; the resulting cancellation will lessen the wave-making component of resistance. A major objective of ship hydrodynamicists is to design hull forms that maximize this benefit. One evident result of their efforts is the underwater bulb often attached to the bows of ships. The purpose of the bulb is to produce a wave that will tend to cancel the ordinary bow wave.

Eddy making by appendages such as rudders and the brackets that support propeller shafts is usually a minor contributor to a hull's resistance to forward motion. It is minimized by giving the appendages airfoil shape and by orienting them, if possible, so that approaching water will have a low angle of attack.

Aerodynamic resistance usually receives much less attention in ship design than hydrodynamic resistance. The aerodynamic contribution to total resistance is small under most circumstances. On occasions when it is not small, as with an exceptionally strong wind from ahead, the resulting waves are likely to require a voluntary reduction in ship speed. The slowing caused by the wind is thus likely to pass unnoticed. The rounding and sloping of deckhouse surfaces is about the only attempt made to design for minimal air resistance.

DETERMINATION OF PROPULSIVE POWER BY MODEL TESTING

The power required to propel a ship is proportional to its speed times the resistance to its movement. The ability to predict resistance is therefore the essential ingredient in predicting the propulsive power to be required by a prospective ship. For many years hydrodynamic researchers have sought a method for calculating this resistance from first principles, but so far they have not produced a generally practicable method. Estimates can be made based on experience with existing ships or standard models, but the favoured way of making a prediction during design is to test a model of the proposed ship.

Model testing consists of towing a precisely made model of the hull at a precisely controlled speed, in calm water, while measuring the force required to tow it. The essential link between model and ship is obtained by operating the model at the same Froude number as the ship. This number, named after the English naval architect William Froude, is a dimensionless ratio given as

$V/(g\,L)^{0.5}$, in which V is the speed, g the acceleration of gravity, and L the waterline length. At this common reference point the wave patterns developed by the ship and by the model are the same, and residuary resistances per ton of displacement also are the same. Unfortunately, equality of Froude numbers means a gross inequality in Reynolds numbers, causing a serious mismatch between the frictional resistances of model and ship. The technique of scaling from model to ship therefore must follow a somewhat devious path whose principal steps are as follows: (1) Total resistance of the model is measured. (2) Frictional resistance of the model is calculated, using data and techniques published by the International Towing Tank Conference. (3) Residuary resistance for the model is found by subtracting the frictional component from the total. (4) Residuary resistance for the ship is taken to be the same, per ton of displacement, as for the model. (5) Frictional resistance for the ship is calculated. (6) Total resistance is obtained by adding the resistance components found in steps 4 and 5.

SHIP MANEUVERING AND DIRECTIONAL CONTROL

A ship is said to be directionally stable if a deviation from a set course increases only while an external force or moment is acting to cause the deviation. On the other hand, it is said to be unstable if a course deviation begins or continues even in the absence of an external cause. A directionally unstable ship is easy to maneuver, while a stable ship requires less energy expenditure by its steering gear in maintaining a set course. A compromise between extremes is therefore desirable. In a rough sense, directional stability or instability can be determined by examination of the ship's underwater profile. If the area of the hull and its appendages is concentrated toward the aft end, then the ship is likely to be directionally stable.

Neither stability nor instability obviates the need for devices to maintain a course or to change it on command. The near-universal gear for such directional control is a rudder (or rudders) fitted to the stern and activated by an electrohydraulic steering engine mounted within the hull just above. The rudder is an appendage that has a cross section much like an airfoil and that develops lift when it is turned to produce a nonzero angle of attack relative to the water. The lift produces a turning moment around a point that is located somewhere along the mid-length of the hull.

For a given angle of attack, rudder lift is proportional to the square of the water velocity relative to the rudder. Therefore, the preferred position for a rudder is within the high-velocity wash generated by a propeller. In the case of a multipropeller ship, multiple rudders may be fitted (one behind each propeller) in order to take advantage of high water velocity. In addition, a ship that must maneuver well while backing is often fitted with a pair of "flanking rudders" for each propeller. These are positioned forward of the propeller, one on each side of the shaft.

Maneuvering at very low speeds is a special problem, since low water velocity means insufficient lift developed by the rudder. If the rudder is positioned directly behind a propeller, then a few seconds of high propeller speed can develop lift sufficient to push the stern sideways before generating significant forward motion of the hull. Pushing the stern sideways is tantamount to changing the direction of the hull, but this expedient is often not sufficient for low-speed maneuvering. For this reason, many ships are fitted with a "bow thruster," a propeller mounted in a transverse tunnel near the bow. This thruster can push the bow sideways without producing forward motion. If a similar thruster is fitted near the stern, a ship can be propelled sideways—or even rotated in place, if the two thrusters act in opposite directions.

SHIP MOTIONS IN RESPONSE TO THE SEA

In maneuvering, a ship experiences yaw (rotation about a vertical axis) and sway (sideways motion). More generally, motions are possible in all six degrees of freedom, the other four being roll (rotation about a longitudinal axis), pitch (rotation about a transverse axis), heave (vertical motion), and surge (longitudinal motion superimposed on the steady propulsive motion). All six are unwanted except in the special circumstance where yaw is necessary in changing course.

Roll is probably the most unwanted of all, since it produces the highest accelerations and hence is the principal villain in seasickness. It can be described as a forced vibration, since the mass, damping, and restoring force typical of any mechanical vibrating system are present. However, attempts to find the natural frequency of a rolling ship through analysis are far from simple, because the coefficients of the fundamental equation are themselves a function of frequency. Further, the mass term must include a rather indefinite amount of water that moves with the ship as it rolls, and there may be coupling between roll and one of the other motions. Nonetheless, natural rolling periods can be found approximately from simplified formulas. Rolling is most severe when the period of encounter with a major part of a wave spectrum equals the roll period.

Many ships are fitted with "bilge keels" in an attempt to dampen roll. These are long, narrow fins projecting from the hull in the area where the bottom of the hull meets the side. Bilge keels are effective in reducing roll, but they are much less effective than other measures. The most effective are antiroll fins that extend transversely from the side of the ship for perhaps 10 metres (30 feet) and are continuously rotated about their axes to develop forces that oppose the roll. Among the sizable costs associated with these fins is the necessity to retract them within the hull when the ship is to be docked.

Pitch is simply roll about a different axis, but consequences and solutions are different. Because a ship is much longer than it is wide, an angle that may seem trivial when it measures roll may lift the bow out of the water when it measures pitch. When the period of encounter with head seas is close to the natural pitching period of the hull, slamming of the bow and cascading of waves upon the forward decks are possible consequences. The most common response to such a hazard is slowing the ship to avoid the resonance. Experiments have been made with anti-pitching fins, but they have not entered into general practice.

The study of ship interaction with surface waves has seen intense effort by hydrodynamicists, since it is a difficult field in which to extract meaningful results from theory while being one where the benefits of solutions are great.

STRUCTURAL INTEGRITY

The simplest structural description of a ship is that its hull is a beam designed to support the numerous weights that rest upon it (including its own weight), to resist the local forces produced by concentrated weights and local buoyant forces, and to resist the several dynamic forces that are almost certain to occur. As with any structure, stresses at all points must remain below the limits allowable for the construction material. Likewise, deflections both local and overall must be kept within safe limits.

In a long-favoured application of beam theory to the design of a ship's hull, the ship is assumed to be supported by a quasi-steady wave (i.e., not moving with respect to the ship) of a length equal to the length of the ship and one-twentieth of this length in height. The ship is taken to be supported by wave crests located at its bow or stern or by a single crest at its mid-length. The hull length is divided into 20 segments, and the weights and buoyant forces within each segment are carefully tabulated. The difference between the sum of all weights and the sum of all buoyant forces within each segment is treated as a load uniformly applied over the segment. The 20 loads are then plotted as a function of position along the hull, and the resulting curve is integrated over the entire ship's length to give what is known as the shear curve. In turn, the shear curve is integrated over the length to give the bending moment curve—a curve that usually has its maximum near mid-length. A value for bending stress can then be obtained by dividing the maximum bending moment by a beam section modulus of the hull structure, which is calculated from a detailed structural plan. For protection against loads neglected in the analysis, such as dynamic wave loads, ample design margins are employed in the calculations.

Since about 1990 the quasi-static treatment of wave loading, as described above, has been recognized as inaccurate. The preferred treatment has become one of finding a still-water (i.e., level sea surface) bending moment, then adding to it a wave-bending moment found by an empirical formula and based only on the size and proportions of the ship. Coefficients in the formula are based on data obtained from at-sea measurements and from tests of structural models; as a consequence, the formula has been found to give predictions that seem to be in satisfactory agreement with reality. The formula is published among the rules of the classification societies that govern the design of commercial ships.

Nevertheless, although a single formula may serve well for ships of typical configuration in sea conditions encountered in typical service, it is not sufficient for all ships in all circumstances. For this reason, research continues into the interactions between the sea and floating structures, the goal being to be able to calculate a load resulting from any interaction between the sea and a floating body. The task is difficult because the analyst must be able to calculate the motion of a ship as caused by waves, the effect on waves of the motion of the ship, and buoyant, damping, and inertial forces present. Such a task would be impossible without extensive at-sea measurement and model testing and without the use of major computing resources. The computing resources became generally available in the 1970s and encouraged efforts that continued well into the 21st century.

Interactions between waves and hull also may occur in a dynamic mode. An obvious example lies in the impact between moving wave and moving hull. Generally, the results of this impact are of small consequence, but the slamming that can occur in rough weather, when the bow breaks free of the water only to reenter quickly, can excite "whipping" of the hull. Whipping is a hull vibration with a fundamental two-noded frequency. It can produce stresses similar in magnitude to the quasi-static wave-bending stresses. It also can produce very high local stresses in the vicinity of the reentry impact.

Another wave-excited hull vibration that can produce significant stress is known as springing. The cause of springing is resonance between the frequency of wave encounter and a natural vibratory frequency of the hull.

Slamming and the consequent whipping can be avoided by slowing or changing course, but springing is more difficult to avoid because of the wide range of frequencies found in a typical sea state. Fortunately, springing has not been identified as a cause of any known structural failure.

The traditional ship hull structure consists of a keel, transverse frames, and cross-ship deck beams that join the frame ends—all supporting a relatively thin shell of deck, sides, and bottom. This structural scheme, which became prevalent with European ships during the Middle Ages, has continued into the age of steel shipbuilding. However, it has a significant drawback in that the frames and deck beams contribute nothing toward resisting longitudinal bending. Frames that run longitudinally do contribute to such resistance and thus permit thinner shell plating. This scheme of framing is strongly favoured in applications where weight saving is important. However, longitudinal frames require internal transverse support from bulkheads and web frames—the latter being, in effect, partial bulkheads that may extend only three to seven feet in from the shell. This requirement obviously reduces the weight advantage of longitudinal framing but not enough to negate the advantage entirely. Web frames also have the drawback of interfering with some uses of interior space, and as a consequence the simple transverse system of framing continues to be employed in many ships.

PROPULSION AND AUXILIARY MACHINERY

At the beginning of the 20th century the near-universal ship-propulsion device was the reciprocating steam engine, furnished with steam from fire-tube boilers in which coal-combustion gases passed through tubes immersed in water. Turbine steam engines, fuel oil, watertube boilers (water within the tubes, combustion gas outside), and diesel engines were first employed in the decade before World War I. Refinements of these innovations continued through the middle third of the century, with the diesel engine gradually supplanting steam for commercial ship propulsion. The sharp increases in petroleum prices in the 1970s gave added significance to diesel's prime advantage—its superior energy efficiency. The resultant saving in fuel cost was large enough to give the diesel engine the preeminent status in commercial ship propulsion that the reciprocating steam engine had enjoyed in 1900.

DIESEL

The diesel engine appears in two distinct types, the medium-speed engine and the low-speed engine. Both operate on the same principles, but each has its own attractions for the ship designer.

The medium-speed engine, characterized by rated speeds in the range of 400–600 revolutions per minute, is in practically all cases a four-stroke engine supercharged by exhaust-driven turbochargers. Power output is proportional to the product of speed and cylinder displacement, and engine size and weight is roughly proportional to cylinder displacement. For a given output, the medium-speed engine is lighter and more compact than the low-speed alternative, and it is usually lower in initial cost. On the other hand, its higher speed nearly always demands a speed-reducing gear between the engine and propeller— a component that is usually unnecessary with low-speed engines. Other handicaps of the medium-speed alternative are a greater number of cylinders for a given power rating and a specific fuel rate (weight of fuel burned per unit of output) that is typically higher than with low-speed engines. On the whole, medium-speed engines are favoured where a particularly heavy or tall engine would be inappropriate and where a lower first cost would outweigh the higher fuel cost.

The low-speed engine is characterized by rated speeds in the range of 80–120 revolutions per minute. In all cases it is a two-stroke engine supercharged by exhaust-gas turbochargers. Whereas medium-speed engines are widely employed ashore, the low-speed engine is almost exclusively a marine engine that is designed to match efficient propeller speeds without recourse to a speed-reducing gear. The consequence of low speed is a longer piston stroke and greater cylinder bore, albeit with fewer cylinders; the net result is a heavier engine, with a specific weight (weight per unit of output) of about 40 kg (88 pounds) per kilowatt—in contrast to a typical figure of 20 kg (44 pounds) per kilowatt for a medium-speed engine. Nevertheless, low speed and large individual cylinder displacement convey advantage to the low-speed engine, since these features allow the lowest-quality—and hence cheapest—fuel to be burned. Even finely powdered coal and coal-oil slurries have been burned in these engines on an experimental basis.

Height, in particular, is a limiting feature of the low-speed engine. In some types of ship, the extra machinery space will interfere with cargo or passenger space.

High-speed engines, with rated speeds of 900 to 1,200 revolutions per minute, are used in a few cases in ships, but engines of this class are almost always found in small craft such as tugs, fishing vessels, and high-speed ferries.

COMBINATIONS OF MACHINERY

Advantage can sometimes be gained by forming a propulsion plant from disparate elements. A memorable example was the *Titanic*, which was built in the early days of steam turbine propulsion. The *Titanic* was propelled by a pair of reciprocating steam engines that exhausted their steam into a single steam turbine. This technique was known as turbocompounding. Turbocompounding, in the guise of turbocharging, is common in diesel technology. Absent an excessively long stroke, a diesel cylinder cannot fully expand its working fluid. One remedy is to exhaust the cylinder gas into a turbine that drives a compressor that in turn supplies the cylinder charge at high pressure. The major benefit of turbocharging is an increase in the power output of the engine without an increase in its size, save for the small increase that the turbocharger represents. In some instances the cylinder exhaust gas contains more energy than the turbocharger requires, and the surplus may be applied to a second turbine whose output is added to that of the engine's crankshaft. Such an arrangement is most likely to be found with low-speed engines in ships built since 1980.

Gas turbines also have been combined with diesel engines as independent units—i.e., supplied with their own fuel and working fluid rather than with diesel exhaust gas. This provides the opportunity to combine the high efficiency of a diesel for cruising speeds with the high output of the comparatively light gas turbine when bursts of speed are needed. Such needs rarely exist among commercial vessels, but combined diesel and gas is appropriate for some military vessels.

GAS TURBINE AND NUCLEAR POWER

The gas turbine engine, essentially a jet engine coupled to a turbine that is geared to a propeller shaft, appeared to have found a niche in commercial ship propulsion about 1970. However, the fuel price increase of the 1970s, which gave diesel its dominance over steam, gave it dominance

The USS North Carolina, *a nuclear-powered attack submarine, at its commissioning ceremony.* U.S. Navy photo by MC3c Kelvin Edwards

over gas as well, and the niche for the latter suddenly disappeared. On the other hand, the gas turbine remains the principal propulsion engine among naval combat vessels because of the high power that can be produced from very low weights and volumes of machinery.

Steam propulsion survives in certain naval vessels—particularly submarines, where the heat source is a nuclear reactor. Extreme cruising range and independence from an air supply are advantages of using nuclear energy as the heat source in naval propulsion, but these advantages are of little merit in commercial shipping. A few prototype cargo ships with nuclear propulsion were built in the 1960s, but they did not lead to commercial application.

ELECTRIC DRIVE AND INTEGRATED MACHINERY PLANTS

Power is usually transmitted from propulsion engine to propeller by means of mechanical shafting. If the engine is a steam or gas turbine, or a medium-speed diesel engine, a speed reducer will be essential in order to match the most efficient engine speed to the most efficient propeller speed. The usual means for accomplishing this is mechanical gearing, but electrical transmission, with a propulsion motor running at a fraction of the speed of a propulsion generator, is an alternative.

Direct-current transmission is occasionally used because it allows propeller speed and engine speed to be completely independent. Alternating-current transmission with synchronous propulsion motors also is used, usually in high-powered propulsion plants because it avoids the commutation problems that handicap high-power direct-current machinery. Exact electrical synchronization of motor speed with generator speed is required, but the mechanical speeds need not be the same. The speed ratio between motor and generator is established by the number of poles in each machine, just as the respective number of teeth establishes a ratio between mating gears.

Electrical transmission was rarely applied to ships built between 1935 and 1970, but it enjoyed a revival of popularity after that. The impetus was the development of thyristor-based frequency converters for alternating-current power, along with the continuing recognition that electrical transmission offers a flexibility that is difficult to match with mechanical transmission. As examples of the latter point, power from a propulsion generator can be used for cargo handling, and a single generator can drive motors on several shafts. The frequency converters are a means of varying synchronous motor speed while frequency at the power source remains constant.

The typical electric-drive ship is a passenger cruise liner with twin propellers driven by synchronous alternating-current motors and powered by an array of medium-speed diesel engines driving synchronous generators. The engine-generators run at a constant 450 revolutions per minute, feeding 60-hertz current to a single bus. All power needs for the ship come from this bus, giving rise to the term *integrated machinery plant*. Power for the propulsion motors passes through thyristor-based frequency changers; by changing propulsion frequency, these devices regulate propeller speed while all other power users continue to receive 60 hertz from the main system.

CHAPTER 6

SHIPBUILDING

S hip construction today is a complicated compound of art and science. In the great days of sail, vessels were designed and built on the basis of practical experience; ship construction was predominantly a skill. With the rapid growth and development of the physical sciences, beginning in the early 19th century, it was inevitable that hydrodynamics (the study of fluids in motion), hydrostatics (the study of fluids at rest), and the science of materials and structures should augment the shipbuilder's skill. The consequence of this was a rapid increase in the size, speed, commercial value, and safety of ships.

THE SHIPYARD

The wooden ship was constructed on a building berth, around which timbers and planking were cut and shaped and then fitted together on the berth to form the hull. A similar practice was followed with iron vessels and, later, with the earlier steel ships, as these tended to be replicas of wooden hulls. Gradually iron came to be used more effectively in its own right, rather than as a substitute for timber. The berth or slipway from which the vessel is launched is an assembly area, rather than a ship construction site. In many shipyards the number of launching berths has been reduced to increase the ground area available for prefabrication sheds. Greater ease of fabrication means that, despite the reduction in the number of berths, more ships can be built and construction costs lowered.

ORGANIZATION

A shipbuilder undertakes to deliver to the client by a certain date and for a stated sum a vessel with specific dimensions, capabilities, and qualities, a vessel that has been tested on trial and is ready for service. The function of a shipyard is the production of completed ships in accordance with the shipbuilder's undertakings. The raw materials for construction and finished items to be installed onboard are delivered there. The labour force in the yard consists of various workmen—steelworkers, welders, shipwrights,

Boat production in a shipyard. Flying Colours Ltd/Digital Vision/ Getty Images

blacksmiths, joiners, plumbers, turners, engine fitters, electricians, riggers, and painters.

Management is headed by a chairman and a board of directors, consisting usually of about 6 to 12 members from the technical, commercial, and secretarial departments, with one or more representing outside interests. The chief departments are the design, drawing, and estimating offices, planning and production control, the shipyard department—responsible for construction up to launching—and the outside finishing department, which is responsible for all work onboard after launching. Other departments are responsible for buying and storekeeping and the yard maintenance.

The construction of the hull is only one of a shipbuilder's responsibilities. As soon as a contract is placed, he must negotiate with subcontractors for the supply of items that shipyards do not produce—the electric power plant, propulsion machinery, shafting and propellers, engine-room auxiliaries, deck machinery, anchors, cables, and furniture and furnishings. Production planning and control is therefore a complex undertaking, covering subcontracts, assembly, and installation, in which costs must be kept as low as possible.

LAYOUT

In general, a shipyard has few building berths and uses extensive areas around them for the construction of large components of the steel hull. Building berths slope downward toward the waterway, to facilitate launching. Building basins, or dry docks, are sometimes used for the construction of very large vessels, because it is convenient to lower, rather than to lift, large assemblies, and this method also eliminates problems associated with launching. Extensive

Container ships being built in a dry dock at the Hyundai Heavy Industries company stockyard in South Korea. Bloomberg via Getty Images

water frontage for the building berths is unnecessary. The main requirement is a site of considerable depth, rather than width, with a large area extending inland from the berths. Steel plates and sections are delivered to the shipyard at the end of the area farthest from the berths. There they are stored in a stockyard and removed, as needed, for cleaning, straightening, shaping, and cutting. Separate streams of plates and rolled sections converge toward the prefabrication shop, where they are used to build structural components or subassemblies. The subassemblies are transported to an area nearer the berths, where they are welded together to form large prefabricated units, which are then carried by cranes to the berth, to be welded into position on the ship.

PLANNING

Delivery of a completed ship by a specified date requires careful planning. Following the introduction in the United States of the critical path method of planning and control by the E.I. du Pont de Nemours and Company about 1959, new techniques were adopted in many shipyards.

The critical path method is the basis of network analysis, which is used in planning complex production projects. The network, and information derived from it, is used for overall planning of a project and also for detailed planning with production progress control. The network gives a logical, graphical representation of the project, showing the individual elements of work and their interrelation in the planned order of execution. Each element of work is represented by an arrow, the tail of which is the starting point of activity and its head the completion. The arrows are drawn to any suitable scale and may be straight or curved. An event, which represents the completion of

ISAMBARD KINGDOM BRUNEL

A British civil and mechanical engineer of great originality, Isambard Kingdom Brunel designed the first transatlantic steamer. Born on April 9, 1806, in Portsmouth, Hampshire, Eng., he was the only son of the engineer and inventor Sir Marc Isambard Brunel. In 1825, when work on the Thames Tunnel began under his father's direction, he was appointed resident engineer. He held the post until 1828, when a sudden inundation seriously injured him and brought the tunnel work to a standstill. While recuperating, he prepared designs for a suspension bridge over the Avon Gorge in Bristol, one of which was ultimately adopted in the construction of the Clifton Suspension Bridge (1830–63) in preference to a design by the noted Scottish engineer Thomas Telford.

Brunel made outstanding contributions to marine engineering with his three ships, the *Great Western* (1837), *Great Britain* (1843), and *Great Eastern* (originally called *Leviathan;* 1858), each the largest in the world at its date of launching. The *Great Western*, a wooden paddle vessel, was the first steamship to provide regular transatlantic service. On its maiden voyage, the ship left Bristol, Eng., on April 8, 1838, and arrived in New York City 15 days later—half the time that sailing ships usually took. The *Great Western* displaced 1,320 tons, was 65 metres (212 feet) long, and carried 148 passengers; it had four masts with reduced rigging and paddles driven by two steam engines. Its average speed without sails was 9 knots.

The *Great Britain*, an iron-hull steamship, was the first large vessel driven by a screw propeller. The *Great Eastern* was propelled by both paddles and screw and was the first ship to utilize a double iron hull. Unsurpassed in size for 40 years, the *Great Eastern* was not a success as a passenger ship but achieved fame by laying the first successful transatlantic cable.

Brunel was responsible for building more than 1,600 km (1,000 miles) of railway in the West Country, the Midlands, South Wales, and Ireland. He also constructed two railway lines in Italy and was an adviser on the construction of the Victorian lines in Australia and the Eastern Bengal Railway in India. He worked on the improvement of large guns and designed a floating armoured barge used for the attack on Kronshtadt in 1854 during the Crimean War. He also designed a complete prefabricated hospital building that was shipped in parts to the Crimea in 1855. Brunel died in London on Sept. 15, 1859.

one activity and the beginning of another, is usually indicated by a circle and described further by a number within the circle. But each activity need not be completed before the next activity is begun. The logical order of steelwork in a hull, for example, is: (1) detailed drawings of steelwork; (2) ordering of steel; (3) manufacture and delivery of steel; (4) storing of steel material in stockyard; (5) shotblasting, cleaning, and forming operations; (6) subassembly work; and (7) erection of structure on berth. These operations can be represented on a ladder type of diagram. Many such diagrams—ladder and other types—go toward making up the complete aggregate operation of building a ship. When the proper sequence of operations is decided upon, times must be allocated to each operation to ensure that the workers in charge understand their obligations. Planning, based on realistic estimates of times and costs, must begin at the precontract stage, so that, throughout the building program, a clear plan, with scheduled dates for each major section, is available. Detailed networks must be prepared for each of the major sections, showing dates for completion. The earliest and latest permissible starting and finishing times are indicated for each activity.

The critical path of a project is a series of activities whose duration cannot be increased without delaying the completion of the project as a whole. In large networks there may be more than one critical path. Up to about 100 activities can be dealt with manually but, for more complex cases, the numerical work is done by computer. The spare time available for a series of activities—i.e., the maximum time these activities can be delayed without retarding the total project—is aggregated into a "total float." This is regarded as a factor of safety to cover breakdowns, mishaps, and labour troubles. Intelligent and experienced use of critical path methods can provide information of great value. Savings in production costs depend upon the use that management makes of this information.

FROM CONTRACT TO WORKING PLANS

Before an order is placed, the main technical qualities of the ship are decided upon and a general-arrangement drawing of the vessel, showing the disposition of cargo, fuel, and ballast, and crew and passenger accommodation is prepared. This plan provides a complete picture of the finished vessel. It is accompanied by detailed specifications of hull and machinery. This general-arrangement plan and the specifications form the basis of the contract between shipowner and shipbuilder.

As soon as an order is confirmed, drawing offices and planning departments produce working plans and instructions. Since ships are usually constructed according to the rules of a classification society, the stipulated structural plans are normally submitted to the society for approval. The spacing of bulkheads in passenger ships, for example, must be approved by the appropriate authority. For all ships, passenger and cargo, the approval of the maximum permissible draft must be sought from the classification society. Necessary working drawings include the lines plan and detailed plans of the steel structure—shell plating, decks, erections, bulkheads, and framing—as well as accommodation spaces, plumbing, piping, and electrical installations, and main and auxiliary machinery layout. The planning and production department prepares a detailed progress schedule, fixing dates for the completion of various stages in the construction. A berth in the yard is allocated to the ship, arrangements for the requisite materials, labour, personnel, and machines are made, and precautions are taken to ensure that the many interrelated operations will progress according to the timetable.

THE LINES PLAN AND FAIRING

Traditionally a lines plan, usually a ¼₈ life-size scale drawing of a ship, was used by designers to calculate required hydrostatic, stability, and capacity conditions. Full-scale drawings were obtained from the lines plan by redrawing it full size and preparing a platform of boards called a "scrive board" showing the length and shape of all frames and beams. Wood templates were then prepared from the scrive board and steel plates marked off and cut to size.

A later alternative to the full-scale scrive board, introduced about 1950 and widely adopted, was a photographic method of marking off. The lines plan was drawn and faired (mathematically delineated to produce a smooth hull free from bumps or discontinuities) to a scale of one-tenth full-size by draftsmen using special equipment and magnifying spectacles. The formerly used wood templates were thus replaced by specially prepared drawings, generally on one-tenth scale. Photographic transparencies of these drawings were then projected full size from a point overhead onto the actual steel plate. The plate was then marked off to show the details of construction, such as position of stiffening members, brackets, and so on. This optical marking-off system was much more economical in the use of space and skilled labour than the older method.

Since the 1960s, computers have been used to fair the preliminary lines plan by a numerical method. Faired surfaces can be produced to a specified degree of accuracy and the lines can be drawn by a digitally controlled drawing machine, bringing the process under continuous scrutiny. Computer programs control the plate-burning machines that cut plates to shape and control the cold bending of frames and curved girders. Fairing calculations produce data that can be fed back into a computer to generate hydrostatic and stability data and other information.

FABRICATION AND ASSEMBLY

Before welding came into wide-scale use in the 1930s, every ship was constructed on the building berth. The keel was laid, floors laid in place, frames or ribs erected, beams hung from the frames, and this skeleton, framed structure was held together by long pieces of wood called ribbands. Plating was then added, and all the parts of the structure were riveted together. In other words, the ship was built from the keel upward.

The modern method is to construct large parts of the hull, for example, the complete bow and stern. Each of these parts is built up from subassemblies or component parts, which are then welded together to form the complete bow or stern. These sections of the ship are manufactured under cover in large sheds, generally at some distance from the building berth, before being transported to the berth and there fitted into place and welded to the adjacent section. The advantages of this procedure are that work can proceed under cover, unhampered by bad weather, and the units or component parts can be built up in sequences to suit the welding operations—not always possible at the building berth itself.

LAUNCHING

Apart from certain small craft built on inland waterways, which are launched sideways, the great majority of ships are launched stern first from the building berth. Standing structures called ways, constructed of concrete and wooden blocks, spaced about one-third of the vessel's beam apart, support the ship under construction. The slope of the standing ways—which are often cambered (slightly curved upward toward the middle or slightly curved downward toward the ends) in the fore and aft direction—ranges from 42 to 62 mm per metre (one-half to three-quarters of an inch per foot) of length; ways

The launch of the Queen Mary *in Jarrow-on-Tyne, Eng., in March 1912.* Buyenlarge/Archive Photos/Getty Images

extend from a position near the bow to past the stern and for a certain distance into the water. Over these standing ways is built the launching cradle, which consists of sliding ways on which are built poppets, or supporting structures, of timber to provide support for the hull. Between standing ways and launching ways is a layer of lubricant.

During construction the ship is supported by at least one line of blocks under the keel, with side supports and shores as necessary. As the vessel nears completion, the standing ways are built under it, the sliding ways are superimposed, and the cradle is built up. The weight of the vessel is transferred gradually to the standing ways. The full weight must not be supported by the ways for too long because the thickness of lubricant would be reduced by squeezing and its properties would be adversely affected. It is common to fit launching triggers which, when released at the moment of launching, permit the sliding ways to move over the standing ways.

As a vessel moves down the ways, the forces operating are: its weight acting down through the centre of gravity, the upward support from the standing ways, and the buoyancy of the water. As it travels further, the buoyancy increases and the upthrust of the ways decreases, with the weight remaining constant. As the centre of gravity passes the after end of the standing ways, the moment of the weight about the end of the ways tends to tip the ship stern first. At this position and for some time later, it is essential that the moment of buoyancy be greater than the moment of weight about the after end of the ways, thus giving a moment to keep the forward end of the sliding ways on the standing ways; otherwise there would be concentration of weight at the end of the ways, causing excessive local pressure. Calculations are made to determine the most important factors in launching, namely, the moment at which the stern lifts, the difference between weight and buoyancy when the stern lifts, the existence of a moment against tipping, and the equality of weight and buoyancy before the vessel reaches the after end of the ways to ensure that the cradle will not drop off the end of the standing ways.

The launching of a vessel into a restricted waterway requires the application of a retarding force. Usually piles of chains are laid alongside the sides of the ship to act as drags, and these are secured to chain plates by wire cables, fixed temporarily to the hull. As the vessel slides down the launching ways, the drags come serially into operation after, or sometimes before, the bow has cleared the after end of the ways. Launching can be a hazardous operation. If the lubricant is ineffective, the vessel will not move. If the stern does not lift as the vessel slides down the ways, the ship may tip about the way ends. The bow may sustain damage when it drops into the water at the end of the ways and may damage the slipway when the stern lifts. Excessive loads on the poppets may cause their collapse.

OUTFITTING

After launching, the ship is berthed in a fitting-out basin for completion. The main machinery, together with auxiliaries, piping systems, deck gear, lifeboats, accommodation equipment, plumbing systems, and rigging are installed onboard, along with whatever insulation and deck coverings are necessary. Fitting out may be a relatively minor undertaking, as with a tanker or a bulk carrier, but in the case of a passenger vessel, the work will be extensive. Although fitting-out operations are diverse and complex, as with hull construction there are four main divisions: (1) collection and grouping of the specified components,

(2) installation of components according to schedule, (3) connection of components to appropriate piping and/or wiring systems, and (4) testing of completed systems.

The tendency in planning has been to divide the ship into sections, listing the quantities of components required and times of delivery. Drawings necessary for each section are prepared and these specify the quantities of components required. A master schedule is compiled, specifying the sequences and target dates for completion and testing of each component system. This schedule is used to marshal and synchronize fitting work in the different sections and compartments.

TRIALS

As the vessel nears completion a number of tests are made. The naval architect makes a careful assessment of the weight of the finished ship and checks its stability and loading particulars by reference to data for the ship's lightweight and centre of gravity, obtained from a simple inclining experiment. The inclining test also provides a check on calculations.

Before the official sea trials, dockside trials are held for the preliminary testing of main and auxiliary machinery. Formal speed trials, necessary to fulfill contract terms, are often preceded by a builder's trial. Contract terms usually require the speed to be achieved under specified conditions of draft and deadweight, a requirement met by runs made over a measured course.

It is usual to conduct a series of progressive speed trials, when the vessel's performance over a range of speeds is measured. The essential requirements for a satisfactory measured course are: adequate depth of water; freedom from sea traffic; sheltered, rather than exposed, waters;

and clear marking posts to show the distance. Whenever possible, good weather conditions are sought. With a hull recently docked, cleaned, and painted, sea-trial performance can provide a valuable yardstick for assessing performance in service. Ideally, the ship should be run on trial in the fully loaded condition; but this is difficult to achieve with most dry-cargo ships. It is, however, comparatively simple to arrange in oil tankers, by filling the cargo tanks with seawater. Large vessels with a low displacement–power ratio must cover a considerable distance before steady speed can be attained; hence they need to make a long run before entering upon the measured distance.

CHAPTER 7

HARBOURS

A harbour is any part of a body of water and the man-made structures surrounding it that sufficiently shelter a vessel from wind, waves, and currents, enabling safe anchorage or the discharge and loading of cargo and passengers. The construction of harbours offers some of the most unusual problems and challenges in civil engineering. The continuous and immediate presence of the sea provides the engineer with an adversary certain to discover any weakness in the structure built to resist it.

Giovanni da Verrazano. Kean Collection/Archive Photos/Getty Images

In certain favoured points on the world's coastlines, nature has provided harbours waiting only to be used, such as New York Bay, which the explorer Giovanni da Verrazano described as "a very agreeable location" for sheltering a ship. Such inlets, bays, and estuaries may require improvement by dredging and must be supplied with port structures, but basically they remain as nature made them, and their existence accounts for many of the world's great cities.

SAN FRANCISCO BAY

San Francisco Bay is a large, nearly landlocked bay indenting western California. Actually a drowned river valley running parallel to the coast, it is connected with the Pacific Ocean by a strait called the Golden Gate, which is spanned by the Golden Gate Bridge. San Francisco Bay is 97 km (60 miles) long and 5 to 19 km (3 to 12 miles) wide. Around the bay are San Francisco, Oakland, and a band of contiguous metropolitan subcentres linked by the Bay Area Rapid Transit (BART).

It is extraordinary that the site of San Francisco should have been explored first by land instead of from the sea, for San Francisco Bay is one of the most splendid natural harbours of the world, yet great captains and explorers—Juan Rodríguez Cabrillo (1542–43), Sir Francis Drake (1579), and Sebastián Vizcaíno (1602)—sailed unheeding past the entrance. In 1769 a scouting party from an expedition led by the Spanish explorer Gaspar de Portolá looked down from a hilltop onto a broad body of water; they were the first Europeans known to have seen San Francisco Bay. It was not until Aug. 5, 1775, that the first Spanish ship, the *San Carlos*, commanded by Lieut. Juan Manuel de Ayala, turned eastward between the headlands, breasted the ebbing tide, and dropped anchor just inside the harbour mouth. It is possible that Drake may have entered the bay, but most evidence suggests otherwise.

Settlers from Monterey, under Lieut. José Joaquin Moraga and Rev. Francisco Palóu, established themselves at the tip of the San Francisco peninsula the following year. The military post, which remained in service as the Presidio of San Francisco until 1994, was founded in September 1776, and the Mission San Francisco de Asis, popularly called the Mission Dolores, was opened in October.

Almost half a century later, a village sprang up on the shore of Yerba Buena Cove, 3 km (2 miles) east of the mission. The pioneer settler was an Englishman, Capt. William Anthony Richardson, who in 1835 cleared a plot of land and erected San Francisco's first dwelling—a tent made of four pieces of redwood and a ship's foresail. In the same year, the United States tried unsuccessfully to buy San Francisco Bay from the Mexican government, having heard reports from whalers and captains in the hide-and-tallow trade that the great harbour held bright commercial possibilities. Richard Henry Dana, whose ship entered the bay in 1835, wrote in *Two Years Before the Mast* (1840) that "If California ever becomes a prosperous country, this bay will be the centre of its prosperity."

The Americans had to wait only another 11 years. After fighting began along the Rio Grande, Capt. John B. Montgomery sailed the sloop of war *Portsmouth* into the bay on June 3, 1846, anchored in Yerba Buena Cove, and later went ashore with a party of sailors and marines to raise the U.S. flag in the plaza. On Jan. 30, 1847, Yerba Buena was renamed San Francisco.

Because natural harbours are not always at hand where port facilities are needed, engineers must create artificial harbours. The basic structure involved in the creation of an artificial harbour is a breakwater, sometimes called a jetty, or mole, the function of which is to provide calm water inshore. Locations for artificial harbours are of course chosen with an eye to the existing potential of the coast; an indentation, however slight, is favoured. Yet it has often been found justifiable on economic or strategic grounds to construct a complete harbour on a relatively unsheltered coastline by enclosing an area with breakwaters built from the shore, with openings of minimum width for entry and exit of ships.

HARBOURS OF THE ANCIENT WORLD

Improvements to natural harbours and construction of artificial harbours were undertaken in very ancient times. There is no conclusive evidence for the date or locality of the first artificial harbour construction, but it is known that the Phoenicians built harbours at Sidon and Tyre in the 13th century BCE.

The engineers of those days either knew or thought little about conservancy even as applied to the ports they

The harbour at historic Sidon, present-day Lebanon. © age fotostock/SuperStock

constructed. Evidence is to be seen in the once thriving ports around the shores of the Mediterranean that now are not merely silent ruins but seem so far from even sight of the sea that it is difficult to imagine the presence of seagoing ships at the wharves, the alignment of which can occasionally be traced in the fertile alluvial land now occupying the site. Ephesus, Priene, and Miletus, on the Aegean shores of Asia Minor, are examples of this type of harbour disappearance, the destructive agent in each of these cases being the picturesque Meander (now the Menderes) River, whose creation of new land from the sea is readily perceivable from high ground adjacent to the river mouth. The formation of further bars is proceeding visibly—and, as there is currently no port in the vicinity whose livelihood can be threatened, it is interesting to speculate how far out to sea this process will ultimately continue in the course of the next millennium or so.

At Side, facing the island of Cyprus, the remains of an ancient breakwater, built to protect the anchorage, can still be seen, but the area enclosed between it and the advancing shoreline is now not a stone's throw wide. In this case, not only the river in the vicinity but also littoral drift, (the movement of sediments by a current parallel to the coast), which produces and maintains extensive beaches to the east and the west, must be held partly responsible for the scale of siltation.

Of many of the ancient port structures, no physical trace remains, but knowledge of the fact that they existed and even a measure of technical description has come down through the written word. With these descriptions and the monuments that still remain, some picture may be formed of the work undertaken by the maritime civil engineers of ancient times.

Given the frailty of the craft for which they were providing, shelter from the weather was the prime consideration; and much effort was devoted to the construction of breakwaters, moles, and similar enclosing structures. Cheap labour was abundant, and the principal material used was natural stone. Surviving structures built in this way are likely to give an appearance of indestructibility, which occasionally attracts favourable comparison with the lighter, more rapidly depreciating modern structures. It is not, however, necessary to credit the engineers of antiquity with a conscious intention to build forever. Given the materials they had to use and the purposes they were implementing, they could do little else; moreover, because there was no rapid pace of advance in the development of ships or land transport, they were undisturbed by the shadow of obsolescence. In the modern age, far from wanting to build forever, the port engineer has to be careful to avoid saddling posterity with structures that may long outlast their usefulness and turn into liabilities. The modern balance between excessive durability and dangerous frailty is one that the ancients never had to strike.

Aided by the characteristics of the material they employed, the ancients constructed maritime works on a scale that is certainly remarkable to this day. Interesting technical practices included the use by the Romans of the semicircular arch in constructing moles or breakwaters, an arrangement that allowed a measure of ingress and egress by the sea to produce a beneficial scouring action in the harbour. The Romans underpinned their structures with timber piling and frequently resorted to the construction of cofferdams (watertight enclosures) that they could dewater by the employment of Archimedean screws and waterwheels. This practice enabled them to carry out much of their foundation work in the dry; and the use of their famous hydraulic cement, pozzolana, gave their structures a durability far exceeding that afforded by the lime cement available to their predecessors.

Among the more interesting harbours of the ancient world are Alexandria, which had on the island of Pharos the first lighthouse in the world; Piraeus, the port of Athens; Ostia, the port of Rome; Syracuse; Carthage, destroyed and rebuilt by the Romans; Rhodes; and Tyre and Sidon, ports of the earliest important navigators, the Phoenicians.

BREAKWATERS

Because the function of breakwaters is to absorb or throw back as completely as possible the energy content of the maximum sea waves assailing the coast, they must be structures of considerable substance. The skill of the designer of a breakwater lies in achieving the minimum initial capital cost without incurring excessive future commitments for maintenance. Some degree of maintenance is of course unavoidable.

BREAKWATER DESIGN

A common breakwater design is based on an inner mound of small rocks or rubble, to provide the basic stability, with an outer covering of larger boulders, or armouring, to protect it from removal by the sea. The design of this outer armouring has fostered considerable ingenuity. The larger the blocks, the less likely they are to be disturbed, but the greater the cost of placing them in position and of restoring them after displacement by sea action. Probably the least satisfactory type of armour block, frequently used because of its relative ease of construction, is the simple concrete cubic, or rectangular, block. Even the densest concrete seldom weighs more than 60 percent of its weight in air when fully immersed in seawater; consequently, such blocks may have to be as much as 30 tons in weight to resist excessive movement.

Boulders of suitably dense natural rock are generally much more satisfactory and, in a project completed in the United Kingdom in the 1960s, it was found by experiment, and subsequently confirmed in experience, that armouring of this type could be composed of blocks of as little as six to eight tons to resist the action of waves up to 5 metres (18 feet) in height. The same experiments showed that, to afford the same protection in the same circumstances, concrete blocks of 22 tons would have been necessary.

In such cases, an intermediate layer of smaller blocks or boulders is inserted between the armouring and the inner core to prevent the finer material in the core from being dragged out by sea action between the interstices of the armour—a process that leads to ultimate settlement and possible breaching by overtopping of the breakwater.

The increasing cost and frequent unavailability within economic distance of suitable natural rock has provoked considerable thought to the design of concrete armour units that can, by reason of their shape, overcome the disadvantages of the simple cubic, or rectangular, block. One of the most successful has been the tetrapod, a four-legged design, each leg projecting from the centre at an angle of 109 ½° from each of the other three. Legs are bulbous, or pear-shaped, with the slightly larger diameters at the outer end. These units have the property, when placed, of knitting into each other in such a way that the removal of a single unit without the displacement of several others is almost impossible, while the interstices between them act as an absorbent of wave energy. Weights substantially less than those needed for cubic blocks are adequate in the case of tetrapods in similar storm conditions. The tetrapods can be mass-produced adjacent to the site through the employment of reusable steel forms.

It is usual to construct some form of roadway along the crest of a breakwater, even when this is not required for any other dockside purposes, to facilitate inspection and access for labour, materials, and equipment for damage repairs.

SOLID BREAKWATERS

In certain circumstances, particularly in parts of the world where clear water facilitates operations by divers, vertical breakwaters of solid concrete or masonry construction are sometimes employed. Some preparation of the seabed by the depositing and leveling of a rubble mound to receive the structure is necessary, but it is usual to keep the crest of such a mound sufficiently below the surface of the water to ensure its not becoming exposed to destructive action by breaking waves. Repulsion of the waves by vertical reflection rather than their absorption is the philosophy of protection in all such cases, but it is not possible to state categorically which arrangement produces the most economical structure.

This type of breakwater can be conveniently constructed through the use of prefabricated concrete caissons, built on shore and floated out, sunk into position on the prepared bed, and filled with either concrete or, less frequently, simple rubble or rock filling. A historical example of this arrangement was the Mulberry harbour built by the Allies and floated into position for the invasion of Normandy in 1944. No previous preparation of the seabed was possible, and only partial filling of the caissons had been carried out when the progress of the war rendered further operations unnecessary. Nevertheless, the fact that several of the caissons remained in position basically undamaged for nearly a decade after the invasion on this notoriously stormy coast demonstrated the possibilities of the method.

FLOATING BREAKWATERS

Because of the large quantities of material required and the consequent high cost of breakwaters of normal construction, the possibility of floating breakwaters has received considerable study. The lee of calm water to be found behind a large ship at anchor in the open sea illustrates the principle. The difficulty is that, to resist being torn away in extremes of weather, the moorings for a floating

A steel breakwater floating in the water. Shutterstock.com

breakwater must be very massive. They are therefore difficult to install and subject to such constant chafing and movement as to require substantial maintenance. Another problem arises, especially in areas of large tidal range. The unavoidable—indeed, essential—slack in the moorings may allow the breakwater to ride large waves, so that they pass underneath it carrying a considerable proportion of their energy into the area to be sheltered.

One approach to the problem is based on the concept of causing the waves to expend their energy at the line of defense by breaking on a large, floating horizontal platform.

CHAPTER 8

DOCKS AND QUAYS

Because the principal operation to which harbour works are dedicated is transfer of goods from one transportation form to another (e.g., from ships to trucks), it follows that docks, wharves, and quays are the most important assets of a port.

Ships must lie afloat in complete shelter within reach of mechanical devices for discharging their cargoes. Although in emergencies ships have been beached for unloading purposes, modern vessels, particularly the larger ones, can rarely afford contact with the seabed without risking serious structural strain. The implications of cargo handling, as far as civil engineering works are concerned, do not differ much whether the loading and discharge are effected by shore-based cranes or by the ship's own equipment. In either case, large areas of firm, dry land immediately alongside the ship are required; the engineer must find a way to support this land, plus any superimposed loading it may be required to carry, immediately adjacent to water deep enough to float the largest ship.

The capital cost of such works probably increases roughly in proportion to the cube of the deepest draft of ship capable of being accommodated; thus the economic challenge posed by the increase in the size of modern ships is considerable. The advent of containerization—the packaging of small units of cargo into a single larger one—has not fundamentally altered this problem, except perhaps to reduce the number of separate individual berths required and to increase greatly the area of land associated with each berth. A figure of 8 hectares (20 acres) per berth is freely mentioned as a reasonable requirement. The problem of land support at the waterline remains the same.

GRAVITY WALLS

The solution initially favoured, and indeed predominant for many years, was that of the simple gravity retaining wall, capable of holding land and water apart, so to speak, through a combination of its own mass with the passive resistance of the ground forming the seabed immediately in front of it. To ensure adequate support without detrimental settlement of the wall, to ensure its lateral stability, and to prevent problems of scour, it is necessary to carry

Gravity retaining walls at the mouth of Whitby harbour, northeast England. iStockphoto/Thinkstock

the foundations of the wall below the seabed level—in some cases a considerable distance below. In earlier constructions, the only guide to this depth in the planning stage was previous knowledge of the ground and the acumen of the engineer in recognizing the characteristics of the ground upon seeing it. Many projects were carried out in open excavation, using temporary cofferdams to keep out the sea. In particularly unfavourable or unstable soils, accidents caused by collapse of the excavation were not unknown.

In modern practice, no such project is initiated without exhaustive exploration of the soil conditions by means of borings and laboratory tests on the samples. Continuous monitoring of the soil conditions during construction is also considered essential. Even so, accidents caused by soil instability still occasionally occur.

The material composing the walls is today almost universally concrete, plain or reinforced, according to the requirements of the design. This material has entirely superseded the heavy ashlar (natural rock) masonry at one time used for such construction, when the techniques for the large-scale production of concrete were not so well developed as they are today.

In some circumstances, particularly those in which the water is reasonably clear or the design and soil conditions do not require very deep excavation into the seabed, the construction of quay walls is adopted by means of large blocks, sometimes of stone but generally of concrete, placed underwater by divers. The economics of this method of construction are influenced by the high cost of skilled divers and by the cumbersome nature of diving equipment. The development of lightweight, self-contained equipment, which leaves the diver considerably more mobile, may relieve this problem.

CONCRETE MONOLITHS

The risks and difficulties attendant on the construction of gravity walls have been avoided, in suitable conditions, through the use of concrete monoliths sunk to the required foundation depth, either from the existing ground surface or, where the natural surface slopes, from fill added and dredged from the front of the quay wall on completion. This technique amounts to the construction above the ground of quite large sections of the intended wall, usually about 15 metres (50 feet) square in plan, which are then caused to sink by the removal, through vertical shafts, of the underlying soil. Another lift of wall is then constructed on top of the section that has sunk, more soil is removed, and the process is repeated until the bottom has reached a foundation level appropriate to the required stability. Considerable skill is sometimes necessary in the sinking process to prevent the monoliths (usually provided with a tapered-steel cutting edge to the lowest lift) from listing, an eventuality that can occur if any part of the periphery encounters material that is particularly difficult to penetrate. Differential loading of the high side and special measures to undercut the material composing the obstruction may be necessary.

The shafts through which the excavated material is removed are generally flooded throughout the operation simply from the intrusion of the groundwater; if necessary, this water can be expelled by the use of compressed air. The excavation of difficult material in detail and in the dry can then be undertaken. It is an operation of some delicacy, because the flotation effect of the compressed air adds a further element of instability to the monolith, and a blow (sudden leakage of air) under the cutting edge may result in flooding of the working chamber. When the bottom edge of the monolith has reached the designed level, the excavation shafts are sealed by concrete plugs. The shafts themselves can then be filled, either with concrete or with dry filling to give the final wall the required mass for stability.

Success in this form of construction cannot be guaranteed. In the case of the Western Docks at Southampton, Eng., constructed between World War I and World War II, it was found impossible, except at inordinate cost, to get the monoliths to sink through the opposing strata to the depth required for stability as a retaining wall. It was therefore necessary to reduce the thrust involved in this function by cutting the retained material back to a natural slope and spanning the gap between the back of the monoliths and the top of this slope by means of a reinforced-concrete relieving platform, supported along its other edge on reinforced-concrete piles. This arrangement has served well enough as far as the quay wall itself is concerned, but the maintenance of the natural slope, stone-pitched as a protection against erosion, has been a continuing liability. In addition, the presence behind the quay of the relieving platform constitutes a formidable obstacle to further construction work—e.g., warehouses or multistory transit sheds.

CONCRETE CAISSON WALLS

In situations in which the depth from ground level to the final dredged bottom is not excessive and the material available for retention as reclamation is of good self-supporting qualities, quay walls can be constructed of precast concrete caissons floated into position and sunk onto a prepared bed in the same manner as that described for breakwaters. Care is taken to design caissons able to

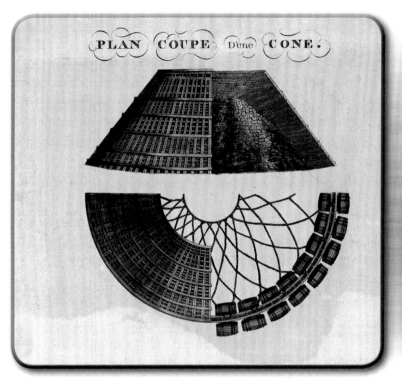

An engraving depicting sectioned views of a wooden caisson to be used in the construction of a breakwater. SSPL via Getty Images

withstand the thrust of the retained material, which is carefully selected for the areas immediately behind the quay wall. The conditions suitable for this form of construction are generally typical of the Mediterranean, where the slightness of the tidal variation keeps the depth required to a minimum.

In all cases of dock wall construction by concrete monolith or caisson, it is the basic structure of the wall that is provided by these means; the final superstructure, above highest tide level, will depend for its detail on the requirements for dockside services, crane tracks, and other elements.

THE PILED JETTY

The high cost, difficulties, and possible dangers of providing dock and quay walls of the kind just described have always encouraged a search for alternative solutions that would eliminate the need for operations on or below the seabed. Of these, the earliest and most obvious is the piled jetty—its piles can be driven from floating craft and the deck and superstructure added thereto, working wholly above water. In regions in which there is a large tidal range, it may sometimes be both advantageous and necessary to take the opportunity provided by extremely low tides to make attachments to the piles for bracing and stiffening purposes. With a reasonable programming of the work, this operation can usually be done without particular difficulty, assuming that the seabed is of a composition reasonably amenable to penetration by piles to a sufficient depth to secure the lateral stability of the structure. Hard rock is not suitable, although some of the more friable rocks can be pierced by steel piles.

Piles may be of timber, reinforced concrete, or steel. Timber is a popular choice if there is a large natural supply. Lateral stiffness and stability can be achieved by using a sufficiently close spacing of the piles in both directions and adequate rigid bracing between the tops, timber being a material readily amenable to the workmanship required. Its chief drawback is lack of durability, particularly in the area between wind and water, although a timber jetty with reasonable maintenance can often resist normal operational obsolescence. There are examples of construction in which the piles are connected together by casting a reinforced-concrete slab around the heads, its soffit (underside) just below lowest water level. By this means, the timber is kept continually submerged, a condition under which its durability is prolonged. On the other hand, in tropical or semitropical waters or waters kept warm by industrial effluents, the use of timber may be inhibited by the presence of marine borers. Timber jetties have a considerable advantage in the comparative ease with which repairs to accident damage or deterioration can be effected.

Reinforced-concrete piled piers and jetties, soundly constructed, exhibit great durability. Attachment to the piles for bracing and similar purposes tends, however, to be more complicated than in the case of timber. This is a disadvantage that applies also to subsequent maintenance and repairs.

THE SHEET-PILED QUAY

An extension of the piled jetty concept is a quay design based on steel sheetpiling, the design becoming increasingly popular with improvements in the detail and manufacture of the material.

DESIGN

Steel sheetpiling consists in essence of a series of rolled trough sections with interlocking grooves or guides, known as clutches, along each edge of the section. Each pile is engaged, clutch to clutch, with a pile previously driven and then driven itself as nearly as possible to the same depth. In this way a continuous, impervious membrane is inserted into the ground. In most designs the convexity of the trough sections is arranged to face alternately to one side and the other of the line along which the membrane is driven, so that a structure of considerable lateral stiffness is built up. At the same time, a measure of flexibility in the clutches allows some angular deviation so that a membrane curved in overall plan is obtainable, a feature of considerable convenience in developing the layout of a series of wharves or quays.

The development of steel sheetpiling over the years has largely been characterized by the increasing weight and stiffness of the sections available from the rolling mills. In one design, the clutch is a separate unit from the main structural element, generally of broad-flanged or universal beam section. In this case, the clutch unit appears in a profile of two grooves, or channels, back to back, each capable of embracing the flanges of adjacent beams, which are thus locked together in a continuous sheet, or membrane, of considerable strength. Each universal section is entered, when pitched for driving, into the clutch on the previously driven section and usually carries the clutch for the next section with it. In another design, made economically possible by the advances in the technique of automatic continuous welding, rolled universal beam sections are welded by one flange into the troughs, or pans, of conventional sheet piles, the composite construction producing a unit of unique strength and stiffness.

The development of steel sheetpiling has kept ahead of the development of hammers capable of driving it, probably because the stiffer the section is, the greater the length of pile that can be incorporated in a design. The combination of heavier section and greater length demands a greater proportion of the energy delivered by the hammer being unproductively absorbed in the temporary elastic compression of the pile, leaving less energy to drive the pile further into the ground. Simply increasing the amount of energy delivered, by using a heavier hammer or a higher drop, does not necessarily provide the solution; it may only result in damage to the head of the pile without achieving greater penetration. This difficulty has been in part overcome by the use of high-strength steel piles. Nevertheless, it is not unknown for a pile to appear to be going down with little or no head damage when it is, in fact, sustaining extensive damage below seabed level that gravely compromises its efficiency as a retaining quay wall. This situation, usually the buckling of a pile, can occur particularly where the material of the seabed contains boulders or similar obstacles to penetration.

The problem has obvious major implications for the construction of quay walls and has provoked much debate among engineers. The skill of the quay designer and the advice of the soil mechanics specialist both contribute to the satisfactory reconciliation of the various conflicting factors outlined in order to achieve the most effective and economical solution.

In the normal design of sheet-piled quay or wharf wall, the sheetpiling itself forms the quay face, although it is generally found advisable to protect the piles from the impact of ships berthing by timber fenders. Vertical timbers at intervals are generally used. Horizontal walings (wooden ridges) between these timbers can also be employed, but they have a disadvantage, particularly at small wharves and with ships having their own protective belting: on a rising tide the beltings become entangled with the walings, occasioning damage or even minor disaster.

The upper part of the sheetpiling, being laterally unsupported on the sea side, is generally anchored back to resist the thrust of the retained soil. This resistance is commonly effected by using tie rods secured to anchors buried in the retained soil itself to a depth that, for reasons of overall stability, is beyond the natural slope line of the soil. As often as not, these anchors are themselves composed of lengths of sheetpiling driven, if possible, below the retained soil into the strata beneath. The mild, or alloy, steel tie rods, coated and wrapped against corrosion, can be carried through the exposed sheetpiling of the quay wall with large retaining nuts on the outside or can be secured to welded attachments at the back of the piling. The latter practice is the more commonly favoured arrangement, largely on account of its more finished appearance. The sheet-piled quay just described is completed by casting a reinforced-concrete cope beam to cover as well as contain the exposed heads of the sheetpiling.

The advantage of this type of quay wall is that the space behind the wall is not occupied—as in the case of the suspended pile-supported deck—by a monolithic, fully structural element, the arrangements of which can be disturbed for subsequent modification of the services layout only at some cost and usually by a potentially complicated design operation. As in the case of a gravity wall, the space can be filled with suitable material that can subsequently be treated, for all intents and purposes, as natural ground in which service ducts can be buried if required. This arrangement is often an advantage in the case of freshwater mains for fire fighting or watering ships because they can thus be protected from frost. Alternatively, it is possible to place concrete-lined service and cable trenches in this material, sometimes conveniently by the use of precast sections, because the ground loads imposed are seldom sufficient to give rise to serious settlement problems.

STRUCTURAL REINFORCEMENT

Identifiable structural loading—arising, for example, from crane tracks—can be supported on reinforced-concrete beams on piles driven through the filling to the strata beneath. Dockside railways, a decreasing requirement because of the transfer of much shore-to-ship delivery to road vehicles, need not necessarily have piled support, because the loading from these can be spread to remain within the bearing capacity of the filling. Some settlement

A sheet-pile quay wall. iStockphoto/Thinkstock

is bound to take place, and the need for compensating by packing up and releveling of the track has the incidental disadvantage of breaking up the surfacing of the quay, which is almost always provided to facilitate quayside access by road vehicles.

Sheet-pile quay walls are readily applicable to sites at which only relatively shallow or medium-depth water alongside is needed. As the required depth increases, a sheet-pile section of sufficient strength and stiffness to hold the retained material without further assistance becomes impractical from the point of view of handling and driving. A solution increasingly favoured is the so-called Dutch quay. In this design, after the line of sheetpiling has been driven using one of the heavier and stiffer sections, the ground behind is excavated for a distance determined by the natural slope of the material to be used as filling and taken down as far as possible to lowest water level. At this level, a reinforced-concrete relieving platform is constructed up against the sheetpiling but with independent vertical support from bearing piles driven through the bottom of the excavation to an appropriate depth. Piles for crane tracks are driven at the same time as these — that is, before the construction of the relieving platform.

Filling material is returned above the relieving platform, and, although the latter now prevents further pile driving in the area, the probability of this being required is remote, whereas the retained load against the sheetpiling is much reduced. The advantages of having filled material behind the sheetpiling for installing services remain. In addition, the relieving platform affords the sheetpiling considerable help in resisting horizontal blows from the impact of berthing ships, and in order to increase this resistance some of the piles supporting the platform are often driven toward the quay face. Reinforced-concrete counterforts between the platform and the sheeting can be an additional help.

DURABILITY

A question that hung over the use of steel sheetpiling in salt water in its early years concerned its durability in potentially hostile conditions. The rate of corrosion, particularly at the waterline or within the tidal range, varied from one locality to another according to the state of the water and the effect of such factors as salinity and industrial effluents. Precoating of the pile with a protective film such as tar or a bituminous paint is of only transient value, requiring regular renewal, and is effective only down to the lowest water level.

The confirmation of the electrochemical basis of much of the corrosion affecting steel sheetpiling led to the development of cathodic protection, a process that has wide application in many other fields, especially shipbuilding. Electrolytic corrosion arises from the passage through the piling of electric currents, causing the pile, or part of it, to become the anode, or positive pole, in what amounts to a galvanic cell, or battery. In such a cell, metal is normally removed from the anode and may reappear on the cathode, or negative pole, which remains unaffected. These currents in sheetpiling may arise from stray leakages from adjacent electrical installations or be generated within the pile itself by differences in the electrolytic conditions at differing levels on the pile.

Cathodic protection is a means whereby cathodic polarity is imposed upon the whole pile, and its operation as an anode (with consequent deterioration) is prevented. This can be done either by supplying from a suitable source—e.g., a battery—an electric current that will overcome and reverse the direction of the naturally generated current or by connecting the piling at intervals to sacrificial anodes of an element—generally aluminum or magnesium—whose atomic relationship to the steel in the piling is such as to generate a current without external assistance. These anodes are buried in the surrounding ground, and care must be taken to ensure full electrolytic continuity between them and the piling to complete the circuit. It is sometimes necessary, in order to ensure electrical continuity between the anode connections in the piling itself, to weld adjacent piles together after driving.

By whatever means cathodic protection is applied, a small liability for operational maintenance arises, either for the continuous supply of the imposed current or for the periodic renewal of the sacrificial anodes. The considerably increased durability of the structure usually justifies this.

ENCLOSED DOCKS

Whenever possible, commercial quays are built open to the tide range to provide maximum freedom for shipping. There are, however, some parts of the world in which the range between low water and high water is so great that the resulting variations in the level of the ship's decks and hatches impose unacceptable disabilities on the handling of cargo. In such circumstances the quay walls may become of such dimensions as to be uneconomical. (The net clear height of the quay walls, disregarding depth of foundations, must span the distance from the lowest seabed level acceptable for navigation at low tide to an adequate freeboard for the coping of the quay wall above the level of the highest high tide. This condition is equally applicable in cases in which only the berths themselves are made to be usable no matter what the stage of the tide.)

The problem can be met by constructing the quays as enclosed docks in which the water level is kept constant and access to the tidal areas is by means of a lock or locks. An obvious condition for the success of such an arrangement is that the strata of the bed under the enclosed dock area be sufficiently impervious to preclude any significant loss of water through the bottom during low-tide conditions. In this way the tidal range, as a limit on the height of the quay walls, can be eliminated.

Apart from the fact that they have gates at each end, the structure of maritime navigation locks and the problems involved in their design are very similar to those of dry docks. Although, in normal usage, a lock is never completely dry, it is essential that it should be designed to be capable of withstanding the stresses imposed by this condition so that it may be possible to dewater the lock completely for inspection and maintenance.

It is common practice to design enclosed docks so that the normal water level maintained is not below the highest likely high tide because the invasion of an enclosed dock by a high tide significantly above the normal water level can be disastrous.

Although enclosed docks are frequently of such an area that they can supply the lockage water lost when a ship passes through the lock without any drop in level that cannot be made up on the next high tide, it is normal to provide a measure of impounding capacity in the form of pumps for lifting additional water from outside into the dock. Such a provision is essential for situations in which it is required to keep the enclosed dock water level above the highest tide.

It has sometimes been possible to accommodate ships of larger draft than originally planned for in large but relatively old enclosed docks. This is done by installing impounding pumps for topping up the water level to give an increased depth.

Enclosed docks generally suffer the operational disadvantage of restricted times of entry and exit because they are subject to a fairly rigid tidal schedule. First of all, the lower the tide level outside, the greater the amount of water lost in the locking operation; and, second, it is seldom economically feasible to maintain full navigation depths in the approach channel to the lock entrance at all levels of the tide. This situation is particularly the case in which enclosed docks are sited adjacent to and operating from a tidal river estuary. The tidal lock at Dunkirk, France, opening to allow the passage of the night channel ferry, which runs on a timetable, is an example of a tidal lock operated whatever the state of the tide.

If possible, the access locks are usually duplicated, lest an accident involving the gates or the structure of the lock put the whole dock area out of operation. Stability calculations of the quay walls within an enclosed dock are important; in older installations such calculations may have been based on the continuing presence of water at the designed normal level, and in the event of a serious failure at the lock—resulting in a considerable drop in the water level—the stability of the quay walls could come into question.

ROLL-ON, ROLL-OFF FACILITIES

An enormous increase in the use of the roll-on, roll-off technique of loading and unloading developed in the late 1960s. The principle of embarking whole vehicles under their own power was not new. The report of Hannibal ferrying his elephants over the Rhône in the 3rd century BCE might be regarded as the earliest example from which the vast amphibious operations of the invasion of Normandy in 1944 were descended. Since the 1960s, however, the spectacular increase in the use of road transport for heavy freight and the increase in handling charges at ports for the loading and discharge of cargo by conventional means have combined to provide the impetus for the rapid commercial development of the roll-on, roll-off technique. In addition, the tendency to assemble machinery at its place of manufacture in larger and larger units has encouraged the development of special transport vehicles, and the economies of moving load and vehicle together from origin to destination can be considerable.

The principal problem for the port engineer is to provide special berthing for the ferry vessels and means of access for vehicles from the shore to the ship's decks. Railcar ferries, involving somewhat similar problems, have been known for some time, but, because of the severer limits on gradients for such vehicles, there has been a tendency to limit the operation of these services to terminals at places where the tidal range is inconsiderable. For the Dover-Dunkirk ferry, opened shortly before World War II, a special enclosed dock was constructed at Dover in which the water level could be kept constant for loading and unloading, while at Dunkirk the entire dock system is totally enclosed, accessible through sea locks.

Many roll-on, roll-off terminals for road services are, by contrast, in tidal water; and, where the tide range is large, access bridges of considerable length are often needed to keep the change of gradient between low and high tide within acceptable limits. The change in the ship's trim between conditions of light loading and full loading creates yet another problem.

At first sight, the solution might appear to be to support the outer end of the link span on a float, or pontoon, so that it would automatically follow the rise and fall of the tide. Several disadvantages of structural detail arise, however, and the system is vulnerable to damage caused by the movement of the pontoon under adverse weather conditions. A means to adjust the height between the span and the supporting pontoon to accommodate changes in a ship's trim is still required; and, therefore, the overall economies of a pontoon are less than might at first be imagined.

Thus it is almost universal practice to support the outer end of the link span from an overhead structure, either through conventional wire-rope hoisting gear or by means of hydraulic rams. The level of the end of the span can thus be continually adjusted, either automatically or by manual control, to match changes in the level of the ship's deck, whether caused by the tide, by the trim of the ship, or by differences in deck levels between one ship and another. Maximum flexibility of access has become increasingly important with the appearance, on some services, of ships with two independent car decks, both of which must be equally accessible to the link span. This situation has sometimes been achieved by the use of double-decker link spans, a technique that has the effect of keeping the length and—unless the span is intended to carry loads on both decks simultaneously—the weight of the span to a minimum.

Maximum advantage of the roll-on, roll-off technique is gained in relatively short sea passages. On longer voyages, the idle road vehicles make the economies questionable. This problem can be overcome to some extent by embarking only semitrailers and leaving the tractive units ashore; the practice has no effect on the terminal details.

BULK TERMINALS

The enormous increase in the marine transit of materials in bulk, with petroleum leading the way, has given rise to the development of special terminals for the loading and discharge of such materials. The principal factor influencing the design of these installations is the still-increasing size of the ships. A single example of the effect of this change on design limits will be sufficient. The "Queen" liners, long the world's largest ships, never drew more than 13 metres (42 feet) of water. Supertankers, on the other hand, when fully loaded, draw up to 22 metres (72 feet). If these ships required berthing structures of the type provided for conventional cargo and passenger liners and if the formula relating the capital costs of such structures to the deepest draft were applied, the cost of building an appropriate berth for such a tanker would reach a figure more than six times the cost of the *Queen Mary*'s old berth. Fortunately, the high mobility of the cargo renders such drastic and expensive measures unnecessary. Heavy capacity access

A container ship being moved into place at a terminal for unloading. Joe Raedle/Getty Images

for individual shore-based vehicles to carry away the cargo is not required, nor does the provision of services for the relatively small crews who man these great ships present any problem. The berthing positions can therefore be sited well out from the shore in deep water, and the structure itself can be limited to that required to provide a small island with mooring devices.

In the case of oil terminals, the link to shore can be a relatively light pier or jetty structure carrying the pipelines through which the cargo is pumped ashore, with a roadway for access by no more than average-size road vehicles, which will probably be used in small numbers or even only one at a time. Because the ship itself carries the pumping machinery for delivering the cargo ashore, heavy mechanical gear for cargo handling is not required.

In the case of bulk carriers bringing solid commodities, such as iron ore, the problem is more complicated.

Hoisting grabs for lifting the ore out of the holds are necessary, even though transit between ship and shore can still be effected by continuous conveyors, corresponding to pipelines. Heavier foundation work is probably necessary at the berthing point to carry this machinery, and, for this reason, ore terminals have not been built as far out in deep water as oil terminals. It seems unlikely that the size of ore carriers will reach anything like the dimensions already attained by supertankers.

The employment of piled structures to meet these requirements is almost universal, and a variety of techniques have evolved for handling and sinking into the seabed the long heavy piles required. At the sites likely to be chosen, penetration by piles may not be easy, particularly in places where most of the reasonably accessible deepwater sites tend to be located on the rockier shores.

One problem that arises is that of shelter in adverse weather conditions. While the ships themselves are reasonably robust, the relatively fragile berthing structures might break up, setting the ship loose, possibly without power immediately available, threatening disaster. As the cost of building breakwaters to protect sites in the depth of water required is likely to be prohibitive, the search has been for natural shelter. In the British Isles the sheltered creeks of the western shores, such as Milford Haven, Wales, have become valuable. Milford Haven had known little shipping other than fishing fleets since the early 19th century, but by the late 20th century it boasted four bulk oil terminals.

Another aspect of the terminals is the need for protection against the effects of unavoidable collision impacts. A slight impact from a vessel of these dimensions, by reason of the large kinetic energy of such a mass, can cause considerable damage to the light berthing structure. Much ingenuity and theoretical analysis have gone into devising fendering systems that will absorb this energy. Some systems use the displacement against gravity of large masses of material disposed pendulumwise in the berthing structure as the energy absorbent; others use the distortion by direct compression, shear, or torsion of heavy rubber shapes or sections; still others rely on the displacement of metal pistons against hydraulic or pneumatic pressure. The common feature of all the devices is that at least part of the energy absorbed is not dissipated but is used immediately to return the ship to its correct berthing position. This feature is not exhibited by the older forms of fenders, which relied on the compression and, in extreme cases, on the ultimate destruction of coiled rope or timber to absorb the impact. A major question is the exact ship velocity to be allowed for, the determination of which is primarily an exercise in probability, balancing the economics of designing to a specified velocity against the cost of repairs after impacts at greater velocities. The key factor is the frequency of such impacts, which can be determined only by experience.

CHAPTER 9

DRY DOCKS

The largest single-purpose structure to be built by the maritime civil engineer is not directly connected with loading, unloading, or berthing but is indispensable to prolonging the life of ships. This is the dry dock, which permits giving necessary maintenance to the underwater parts of ships. The problem of dry-docking is aggravated by the tendency of ships to grow in size by increases in beam (width) and draft (depth below waterline) rather than in length, a process that rapidly renders many of the world's largest dry docks useless for servicing an increasing proportion of the traffic.

A classic example is the King George V Drydock at Southampton, Eng. Opened in 1933, it was 365 metres (1,200 feet) long and 40 metres (135 feet) wide and was capable of accommodating the largest vessels afloat—namely, the two Cunard liners *Queen Mary* and *Queen Elizabeth*, each more than 80,000 tons deadweight. The later supertankers have deadweight tonnages of 135,000 tons and more, within a length of about 400 metres (1,300 feet) but with a beam of about 50 metres (175 feet), which precludes them from entering the King George V dock. The lengthening of a dry dock would be a comparatively simple and economical operation; widening, on the other hand, involves at least the complete demolition of one sidewall and its rebuilding to give the increased clear width to the other wall, assuming space can be made available.

Dry dock workers cleaning the hull of the amphibious assault ship USS Bonhomme Richard. U.S. Navy photo by CMC Joe Kane

Increasing the depth would mean a new dock altogether, but, because tankers generally dry-dock in the unloaded condition in which their draft can be considerably less than that of a conventional ship, this problem has not so far been a practical one.

STRUCTURAL REQUIREMENTS

In a great many cases, the maximum state of stress in a dry dock occurs not when it is carrying the weight of the ship (always considerably less than the weight of the water occupying the dock when flooded) but when it is completely empty and subject to the pressures generated by water in the surrounding ground, particularly under the floor, the support of which may lie at a considerable depth below the level of the adjacent water table. To ensure against any tendency to lift under this pressure, the floor must either have sufficient weight in itself (300 mm, or 1 foot, depth of concrete will resist a little less than 750 mm, or 2 ½ feet, head [depth] of water) or be designed as a structural element capable of transmitting this pressure laterally to the walls of the dry dock, which can then be designed to contribute the additional extra weight required. Obviously an operation involving both the complete rebuilding of one wall of a dry dock and the strengthening of the floor to cover an increase in its span as an inverted arch or beam is almost tantamount to the construction of a complete new dock.

DESIGN

The design of a dry dock probably depends more on ground conditions than does any other engineering structure, with the possible exception of large dams.

Mention has been made of the need in many cases to resist upward pressures under the floor. Apart from the simple solution of using the weight of the dock structure itself for this purpose, which is not economical, devices that have been tried include "pegging" the floor to the underlying strata by means of piles or prestressed anchors and extending the floor slab itself beyond the sidewalls, thereby gaining assistance from the weight of the material filling behind the walls, which are designed to act as retaining walls to this filling. Venting of the floor to relieve water pressure can sometimes be of help provided the volume of water so released is not excessive. If it is, continuous pumping to keep the dock dry will be necessary. On sites in which water pressures do not have to be resisted, the design is generally simpler, and sufficient strength and stiffness to spread the loads from the ships' keels over the underlying ground so as not to exceed the bearing resistance of the latter is the controlling floor-design factor.

The use of dry docks for the building rather than the maintenance of ships is a practice that has been increasingly adopted. Both the building and the launching of a ship in these circumstances can be considerably simplified. The designs of such dry docks are no different from those hitherto described.

ENTRANCES

Dry dock entrances are closed by gates of different designs, of which the sliding caisson and the flap gate, or box gate, are perhaps the most popular. The sliding caisson is usually housed in a recess, or camber, at the side of the entrance and can be drawn aside or hauled across with winch and wire rope gear to open and close the entrance.

An emptied dry dock using retractable gates to hold back the harbour water.
Grant Duncan-Smith/Gallo Images/Getty Images

The flap gate is hinged horizontally across the entrance and lies on the bottom, when in the open position, to be hauled up into the vertical position to close the dock—a process occasionally facilitated by rendering the gate semibuoyant through the use of compressed air.

The ship type of caisson gate, a quite separate vessel floated and sunk into its final position across the entrance, is largely out of favour. Although it was comparatively easy to remove for maintenance and had the further advantage that a spare caisson could be kept in reserve in case of damage, the tie-up of capital is usually found unnecessarily expensive merely as an insurance premium.

The maximum degree of watertightness obtainable between the gate and its seating is essential if continuing and expensive operational commitments for pumping out leakage water are to be avoided. The pressure of the water outside the gate is available to provide a powerful sealing force, but special treatment of the actual contact faces is necessary to make this force fully effective. For a long time it has been held that the only satisfactory arrangement was by the use of a timber lining (generally greenheart) around the contact face on the gate, bearing against stops in the dock structure composed of granite dressed and polished to a high degree of accuracy. The increased expense of such methods and the diminishing number of skilled labourers capable of dressing the granite have led to a search for alternatives. These include such devices as the use of stainless facing bars set in concrete, in place of the dressed granite, and rubber linings on the gates themselves. While these have generally proved effective when first installed, more experience is needed to determine their durability as compared with older methods.

KEEL AND BILGE BLOCKS

Keel and bilge blocks, on which the ship actually rests when dry-docked, are of a sufficient height above the floor of the dock to give reasonable access to the bottom plates. Such blocks are generally made of cast steel with renewable timber caps at the contact surfaces. Individual blocks can generally be dismantled under the ship to allow access to that part of the plates, if required, and can be reassembled to take their appropriate share of the weight after the operation required has been completed. Most modern ships, particularly tankers, are of nearly square section over a large part of their middle length and can be kept upright in dry dock by the support of the bilge blocks under their bilge keels. In the most up-to-date dry docks, the bilge blocks are provided with mechanical means for traversing them across the dock and altering their height by remote control while the dock is still flooded. This arrangement permits them to be adjusted in their correct position according to the shape of the ship while the latter is still just afloat but in contact with the centre-line keel blocks. The economic advantage of this arrangement is considerable because it allows one ship to be removed and another put into the dry dock on the same opening of the gate, whereas under previous practice it would have been necessary to close the dock and pump it out to reset the bilge blocks to the known profile of the next ship. Apart from the time needed, the power consumed in pumping out a large dry dock is a considerable factor.

Because of the increasing number of ships suitable for bilge docking, the use of side shores to keep hulls upright in dry dock is a rapidly dying process, and indeed the altars provided for this purpose in dry docks of more old-fashioned design are often an embarrassment to the accommodation of a modern square-sectioned ship. Frequently this situation is remedied by cutting away some altars, an operation that must be conducted with discrimination because the removal of any quantity of material from the sidewalls may have a damaging effect on their stability.

BASIC CONSTRUCTION TECHNIQUE

Dry docks are usually constructed in open excavation in the dry, shutting out the sea by means of a cofferdam. Sometimes it is found convenient to construct the sidewalls first, in trench, next to remove the loose material between them, and then to lay the floor in stages so as not to endanger the stability of the walls before the floor is in position to give them toe support. Extensive pumping, to keep the excavations from filling with water during construction, is generally necessary.

In one rather unusual case, a dry dock for 240,000-ton tankers was constructed almost wholly under water because large fissures in the rock running through to the sea flooded the site beyond the capacity of any reasonable assembly of pumping equipment. The entire space required for the structure was therefore excavated to formation level by dredging, and the sidewalls were constructed first, using prefabricated concrete caissons sunk into place and filled with concrete. The spaces between adjacent caissons were sealed by filling with concrete in the same way. Stone aggregate, to a depth of 7 metres (23 feet), was then deposited between these walls and consolidated into a concrete floor by a process of grouting in which colloidal cement grout was forced under pressure between the interstices of the aggregate, subsequently setting to form the whole into concrete. A similar process

across the floor at the entrance incorporated a coffer-dam of interlocking steel sheetpiling, which allowed the sill and gate hinge to be constructed in the dry. The gate, of the flap variety already mentioned, was floated and stepped into place by divers after the removal of the cofferdam. Only then was it possible to pump out the main body of the dock, which was completed by laying a reinforced concrete topping over the floor in order to provide a satisfactory working surface.

FLOATING DRY DOCKS

Floating dry docks have the initial advantage that they can be built and fully equipped in shipyard and factory conditions, in which their construction is not subject to unforeseen hazards arising from weather and variations in the ground conditions from those anticipated during design. The floating dock can be towed to the site, moored, and made ready for operation in a comparatively short time. Expenditure on temporary works, often a large fraction of the cost of a fixed dry dock, is also avoided.

Floating dry docks are usually fully self-contained. The sidewalls provide much of the residual buoyancy and stability required to keep the dock afloat when it has been submerged far enough to allow the entry of a ship into the docking space over the main deck. Most of the machine tools and workshop equipment required for all the normal operations of ship repair and maintenance are also housed in the walls as well as the generating plant (usually diesel driven) to supply power for the operation of the dock and its equipment. Traveling cranes, for handling material off and onto the ship, run on the tops of the sidewalls.

A floating dry dock can be moved at relatively short notice to another site, should a long-term change in shipping-traffic patterns dictate a change. This advantage may be more apparent than real, because the large work force required to man it may not be so readily transferable.

Moreover, floating dry docks tend to have large maintenance costs because the steel structure, being continually afloat, requires regular chipping and painting, as the hull of a ship does. The above-water structure presents no particular problem and can generally be given maintenance care without putting the dock out of use. The most vulnerable areas, those immediately adjacent to the waterline, can be reached by careening, a process that involves filling the water ballast tanks along one side to induce a list that lifts those on the other side part of the way out of the water. On completion, the process can be reversed for the other side.

MAINTENANCE

Methods of underwater scaling and painting, or the use of limpet dams with which small areas can be covered with watertight enclosures inside of which people can work under compressed air, allow a limited measure of attention to be given to the bottom plating outside. Occasionally it is necessary to detach one of the sections of the dock, which is usually constructed in separate sections for this reason, and dry-docking it in the remainder, repeating the process until the whole dock has been renovated. This costly and tedious process is resorted to only for compelling reasons.

To give a floating dock sufficient depth of water for submerging the docking blocks below the keel of the ship to be docked, it may be necessary to dredge a berth for it.

The Golden Gate Panama *cargo ship.* Daniel Berehulak/Getty Images

In areas subject to heavy siltation, this dredged area will almost certainly act as a silt trap. Periodic removal of the dock from the berth to allow the latter to be redredged is an additional source of expenditure in such cases. Finally, in places where the tide range is of consequence, special mooring arrangements are necessary to restrain excessive lateral drift of the dock as the mooring chains become slack on low water.

The arrangement of keel and bilge blocks is generally similar to those described for fixed dry docks.

CONCLUSION

Today, as in the past, much of the world's commerce depends upon ships. Ships carry food and textiles; bulk supplies of coal, oil, and grain; complete offshore modules and huge sections of process equipment; automobiles; paper, chemicals, and steel; and machine tools and personal computers. Many giant space launchers journey by water to their launching sites. Ships still transport people as well, though they have largely been supplanted by airliners as transoceanic passenger carriers. Maritime and nonmaritime countries alike depend on a vigorous worldwide shipping industry, and to a great extent the prestige of a state depends on the size and modernity of its maritime fleet. Ships, as well as the onshore facilities designed to maintain them and to load and off-load their cargoes, will continue to be an important factor in the global economy even in the age of jet travel and space exploration.

GLOSSARY

ashlar Hewn or squared stone.

berth The place where a ship lies when at anchor or at a wharf.

bireme A galley with two banks of oars used especially by the ancient Greeks and Phoenicians.

bow The forward part of a ship.

bulkhead An upright partition separating compartments.

buoyancy The upward force exerted by a fluid on a body placed in it.

burtoning A system of handling a ship's cargo by means of a sling rigging between two derricks or masts.

buss A rugged square-sailed boat formerly used especially in herring fishery.

cabotage Trade or transport in coastal waters or airspace or between two points within a country.

caisson A hollow floating box or a boat used as a floodgate for a dock or basin.

caramaran A vessel (as a sailboat) with twin hulls and usually a deck or superstructure connecting the hulls.

carrack A beamy sailing ship especially of the 15th and 16th centuries.

carvel-built Built with the planks meeting flush at the seams.

clinker Having the external planks or plates overlapping like the clapboards on a house.

cofferdam A watertight enclosure from which water is pumped to expose the bottom of a body of water and permit construction (as of a pier).

deadweight A ship's load including the total weight of cargo, fuel, stores, crew, and passengers.

electrohydraulic Involving or produced by the action of very brief but powerful pulse discharges of electricity under a liquid resulting in the generation of shock waves and highly reactive chemical species.

friable Easily crumbled or pulverized.

hull The frame or body of a ship or boat exclusive of masts, yards, sails, and rigging.

hydrodynamics A branch of physics that deals with the motion of fluids and the forces acting on solid bodies immersed in fluids and in motion relative to them.

ingress Entrance.

interstice A space that intervenes between things.

keel The chief structural member of a boat or ship that extends longitudinally along the center of its bottom and that often projects from the bottom.

lateen Being or relating to a rig used especially on the north coast of Africa and characterized by a triangular sail extended by a long spar slung to a low mast.

littoral Of, relating to, or situated or growing on or near a shore, especially of the sea.

lodestone Magnetite possessing polarity.

metacentre The point of intersection of the vertical through the centre of buoyancy of a floating body with the vertical through the new centre of buoyancy when the body is displaced, however little.

pilferage The act of plundering or robbing.

pneumatic Of, relating to, or using gas (as air or wind).

pozzolana Hydraulic cement made by grinding pozzolana (a type of slag that may be either natural—i.e., volcanic—or artificial, from a blast furnace) with powdered hydrated lime.

propulsion The act or process of driving forward or onward by or as if by means of a force that imparts motion.

ribband A long narrow strip or bar used in shipbuilding.

scantling The dimensions of a structural element used in shipbuilding.

scrive board A platform of well-seasoned boards on which are drawn full-size the lines of the body of a ship to be built.

stern The rear end of a boat.

sway An oscillating, fluctuating, or sweeping motion.

thyristor Any of several semiconductor devices that act as switches, rectifiers, or voltage regulators.

trireme An ancient galley having three banks of oars.

viscosity The ratio of the tangential frictional force per unit area to the velocity gradient perpendicular to the direction of flow of a liquid.

yaw A side to side movement.

BIBLIOGRAPHY

Lionel Casson, *The Ancient Mariners: Seafarers and Sea Fighters of the Mediterranean in Ancient Times*, 2nd ed. (1991), and *Ships and Seafaring in Ancient Times* (1994), cover the origins of ships and seafaring from the ancient Phoenicians and Egyptians through the biremes and triremes of the Greco-Roman era. Richard W. Unger (ed.), *Cogs, Caravels and Galleons: The Sailing Ship 1000–1650* (1994; reissued 2000), part of the series *Conway's History of the Ship*, and *The Ship in the Medieval Economy, 600–1600* (1980), cover the evolution of sailing ships in medieval Europe.

Alan Villiers, *Square-Rigged Ships: An Introduction* (2000; first published 1975 as *Voyaging With the Wind*), written by an experienced seaman and trustee of the National Maritime Museum, London, explains the design and handling of fully rigged sailing ships. William L. Crothers, *The American-Built Clipper Ship, 1850–1856* (1997), describes in great detail the design and construction of the great Yankee sailing ships. Hans Konrad Van Tilburg, *Chinese Junks on the Pacific: Views from a Different Deck* (2007), is a history of these traditional Chinese sailing vessels as well as an analysis of Western misunderstanding of Chinese technology and culture.

Stephen R. Fox, *Transatlantic: Samuel Cunard, Isambard Brunel, and the Great Atlantic Steamships* (2003), re-creates the transition in the North Atlantic trade from the sailing packets of the early 19th century to the great steamships of the late 19th and early 20th centuries. Arnold Kludas, *Record Breakers of the North Atlantic: Blue Riband Liners 1838–1952* (2000; trans. from the German), by a former director of the scientific library of the German Maritime Museum, Bremerhaven, traces the quest for speed on the transatlantic route from the *Great Western* to the *United States*.

Marc Levinson, *The Box: How the Shipping Container Made the World Smaller and the World Economy Bigger* (2006), explains the economic changes brought about by containerized shipping since its rise in the mid-20th century. Raymond Solly, *Tanker: The History and Development of Crude Oil Tankers* (2007), with illustrations and photographs, traces the growth of oil tankers as well as their economic and environmental impact.

Harry Benford, *Naval Architecture for Non-Naval Architects* (1991); and Cyrus Hamlin, *Preliminary Design of Boats and Ships* (1989), are books for the nonengineer that give simple explanations of the design process and of marine design principles. D.J. Eyres, *Ship Construction*, 6th ed. (2007), is a standard work covering all aspects of shipbuilding.

Alan E. Branch, *Elements of Shipping*, 8th ed. (2007), is a definitive guide to commercial shipping. Gregory P. Tsinker (ed.), *Port Engineering: Planning, Construction, Maintenance, and Security* (2004), with chapters written by specialists, covers all aspects of planning, building, and maintaining port facilities.

INDEX